OXFORD CENTRE TEXTBOOKS

General editor
Geza Vermes, MA DLitt FBA

Volume I

JSOT Press

The Essenes

According to the Classical Sources

edited by
Geza Vermes
&
Martin D. Goodman

Published on behalf of the
Oxford Centre for
Postgraduate Hebrew Studies
by
JSOT Press
Sheffield

Copyright © 1989 Sheffield Academic Press

Published by JSOT Press
JSOT Press is an imprint of
Sheffield Academic Press Ltd
The University of Sheffield
343 Fulwood Road
Sheffield S10 3BP
England

Phototypeset in 11-point Ehrhardt
at Oxford University Computing Service
and printed in Great Britain
by Billing & Sons Ltd
Worcester

British Library Cataloguing in Publication Data

The Essenes according to the classical
  sources
  1. Essenes
  I. Vermes, Geza, *1924-*   II. Goodman, Martin
  III. Series
  296.8'1

ISBN 1-85075-139-0

CONTENTS

Preface to the Series		vii
Foreword		ix
Abbreviations		x

Introduction 1

I.	The Essenes described by Philo, Josephus and Pliny the Elder	2
II.	The Community of the Dead Sea Scrolls	7
III.	The relationship between the Essenes and the Qumran sect	12
IV.	Essene and Qumran history	14
	Appendix	
1.	The Therapeutae	15
2.	The Therapeutae and the Essenes	16
3.	The Therapeutae and the Qumran Community	17

The Sources 19

1. Philo
    - (a) *Quod omnis probus liber sit* 75–91 — 19
    - (b) *Apologia pro Iudaeis* — 26
2. Pliny the Elder
    - *Natural History* 5. 17, 4 (73) — 32
3. Flavius Josephus
    - (a) *The Jewish War* — 34
        - i. 1. 78–80 — 34
        - ii. 2. 113 — 36
        - iii. 2. 119–161 — 36
        - iv. 2. 567; 3. 11 — 48
        - v. 5. 145 — 48

		(b) *Antiquities of the Jews*	50
		i. 13. 171–172	50
		ii. 15. 371–379	50
		iii. 18. 18–22	54
	(c)	*Life* 10–11	56
4.	Dio of Prusa, in Synesius, *Dio* 3,2		58
5.	Hegesippus, *Hypomnemata*		60
6.	Hippolytus of Rome, *Refutation of all heresies* 9. 18–28		62

Appendix

Philo, *On the contemplative life* 1–2, 11–40, 63–90   75

Bibliography   101

PREFACE TO THE SERIES

In order to facilitate the historical and linguistic study of inter-Testamental and rabbinic literature from the original sources, the Oxford Centre for Hebrew Studies in association with the Sheffield Academic Press is launching a new series entitled, *Oxford Centre Text-Books*. The volumes are intended, and priced, for University and College students and will include Hebrew, Aramaic, Greek and Latin (and occasionally Syriac) texts.

The series is conceived on the combined pattern of, on the one hand, the German *Kleine Texte*, initiated by H. Lietzmann (see also the English *Semitic Studies Series*, edited by R. J. H. Gottheil and M. Jastrow) and the *Loeb Classical Library*, on the other. This implies that in addition to a reproduction of the original works the volumes will contain a facing English translation and brief notes, as well as a fairly full introduction and a reasonably detailed bibliography.

It is hoped that the easy availability, in their totality or in representative excerpts, of some of the basic Jewish writings, will contribute to the spread and advancement of Judaic studies, thus promoting the principal aim of the Oxford Centre.

Geza Vermes
Director of Publications
of the Oxford Centre for Hebrew Studies

FOREWORD

The first volume of the series contains the most important Greek and Latin texts relating to the ancient Jewish sect of the Essenes. Geza Vermes has supplied the main introduction and the bibliography; Martin Goodman is responsible for the notes and introductions accompanying the texts and also for the English rendering of the classical sources or for the revision of existing translations.

The following editions have been used.

Philo	*Q.o.p.* and *V.C.*	L. Cohn and P. Wendland, *Philonis Alexandrini opera quae supersunt*, vol. 6 (1915)
	Apol.	K. Mras, ed., Eusebius, *Werke*, vol. 8, *Die Praeparatio Evangelica*, GCS 43 (1954)
Pliny		C. Mayhoff, *C. Plini Secundi Naturalis Historiae*, vol. 1 (1906)
Josephus		B. Niese, ed., *Flavii Iosephi opera*, 7 vols (1885–95)
Dio		J. De Arnim, *Dionis Prusaensis quem vocant Chrysostomum quae exstant omnia*, vol. 2 (1896)
Hegesippus		E. Schwartz, ed., Eusebius, *Werke*, vol. 2, *Die Kirchengeschichte*, GCS 9. 1 (1903)
Hippolytus		M. Marcovich, ed., Hippolytus, *Refutatio omnium haeresium* (1986).

The editors wish to acknowledge permission from Basil Blackwell to use and adapt translations from A. Dupont-Sommer, *The Essene Writings from Qumran*, translated by G. Vermes (Oxford 1961), and from Walter de Gruyter & Co. to use the text of Hippolytus, *Refutatio omnium haeresium*, edited by M. Marcovich (Berlin and New York, 1986).

Geza Vermes
Martin Goodman

ABBREVIATIONS

Sources

Ant.	Josephus, *Antiquities of the Jews*
Apol.	Philo, *Apologia pro Iudaeis*
CD	Cairo Damascus Rule
Life	Josephus, *Life*
4QFlor.	Florilegium or Midrash on the Last Days
1QH	Hodayoth or Thanksgiving Hymns
1QM	War Rule (from Cave 1)
4QM	War Rule (from Cave 4)
Q.o.p.	Philo, *Quod omnis probus liber sit*
1QpHab	Commentary on Habakkuk
1QS	Community Rule
1QSa	Messianic Rule
1QSb	The Blessings
11QTS	Temple Scroll
Ref.	Hippolytus, *Refutation of all Heresies*
V.C.	Philo, *De vita contemplativa*
War	Josephus, *The Jewish War*

Modern works and periodicals

ANRW	H. Temporini and W. Haase (eds.), *Aufstieg und Niedergang der römischen Welt*
BA	Biblical Archaeologist
CRAI	Comptes-rendus de l'Académie des Inscriptions et Belles-Lettres
DBS	*Dictionnaire de la Bible, Supplément*
DSSE	G. Vermes, *The Dead Sea Scrolls in English*, 3rd ed., 1987
Enc. Jud.	*Encyclopaedia Judaica*
HJP	E. Schürer, rev. G. Vermes, F. Millar, M. Goodman, M. Black, *The History of the Jewish People in the Age of Jesus Christ*, 3 vols., 1973–87

HTR	Harvard Theological Review
HUCA	Hebrew Union College Annual
IDB	*The Interpreter's Dictionary of the Bible*
JE	*The Jewish Encyclopedia*
JJS	Journal of Jewish Studies
JTS	Journal of Theological Studies
JWSTP	M. E. Stone (ed.), *Jewish Writings of the Second Temple Period*, 1984
MGWJ	Monatsschrift für Geschichte und Wissenschaft des Judentums
PBJS	G. Vermes, *Post-Biblical Jewish Studies*, 1975
QIP	G. Vermes, *The Dead Sea Scrolls: Qumran in Perspective*, 2nd ed., 1982
RB	Revue Biblique
RE	Pauly-Wissowa, *Realencyclopädie der classischen Altertumswissenschaft*
REJ	Revue des Études Juives
RQ	Revue de Qumrân
STJ	G. Vermes, *Scripture and Tradition in Judaism*, 2nd ed., 1973
ThZ	Theologische Zeitschrift
ZAW	Zeitschrift für die Alttestamentliche Wissenschaft

Brackets in the Greek text

[ ]	Gap in transmitted text; words inserted are hypothetical
⟨ ⟩	Gap is presumed; words inserted are hypothetical
{ }	Presumed addition; cancellation proposed
( )	Addition of the editor

INTRODUCTION

The discovery in 1947 of the first Dead Sea Scrolls reawakened scholarly interest in the Essenes, one of the four main religious parties of Palestinian Judaism in the inter-Testamental age. Prior to Qumran, the only evidence concerning them came from Greek and Latin sources. Two primary Jewish witnesses, Philo of Alexandria and Flavius Josephus, wrote in Greek; the third, the Roman Pliny the Elder, left a short notice in Latin. All three flourished in the first century A.D. Significant additional sources in classical languages date from the second and the third centuries. The main part of this text-book, intended for University and college classes, consists in an annotated bilingual edition of their accounts. Philo's *De vita contemplativa*, describing the Therapeutae, an Egyptian group of Jewish ascetics related in some way to the Essenes, is given as an appendix.

The designation of the group and the etymology of its name are obscure and controversial. Josephus most frequently refers to its members as *Essenoi*,[1] but also as *Essaioi*.[2] The latter form is the only one used by Philo, whereas Pliny calls them *Esseni*. Philo, whose familiarity with Hebrew and Aramaic was fairly limited, suggests a punning Greek etymology: *hosioi* = the holy,[3] but modern scholarship, whilst disagreeing over its identity, assumes that the Greek and Latin forms transliterate a Semitic term.[4] The derivation most commonly advanced is from the Syriac *ḥase'* = 'pious', the equivalent of *ḥasid* in Hebrew,[5] but the lack of Jewish Aramaic evidence for *ḥsy* in this sense undermines

---

[1] See *Ant.* 13.171–2, 298, 311, 372–3, 378; 18. 11, 18. *War* 2. 119, 158, 160; 5. 145. *Life* 10.
[2] See *Ant.* 15. 371; 17. 346; *War* 1. 78; 2. 113, 567; 3. 11.
[3] *Q.o.p.* 75, 91; *Apol.* 1 = *Praep. ev.* viii. 11, 1.
[4] Cf. PBJS (1975), 9–19; S. Goranson, RQ 11 (1984), 483–98.
[5] Cf. F. M. Cross, *The Ancient Library of Qumran* (1980), 37, n. 1; J. T. Milik, *Ten Years of Discovery* (1959), 80, n. 1.

the argument. The difference between *Essaioi* and *Essenoi/Esseni* is explained through the association of the former to the emphatic and the latter to the absolute form of the Aramaic plural: *ḥsy'–ḥsyn*.[6] Since the Qumran finds, an etymology, current in the nineteenth century, has been revived, connecting the name with *'sy'* = healers.[7] The theory is founded on Josephus's assertion that the Essenes were concerned with cures,[8] on Philo's understanding of the word *therapeutai* as designating 'healers' of soul and body,[9] and on ideas relating to medicine, current in inter-Testamental Judaism and in the New Testament.[10]

The Essenes are never alluded to directly either in the New Testament or in Talmudic literature. Numerous attempts have been made to identify obscure rabbinic references as relating to this sect, but all of them remain purely speculative.[11]

In order to set out the evidence as objectively as possible, the information collected from the classical sources and from the Dead Sea Scrolls is first presented separately. The two pictures are then subjected to a systematic comparison. The introduction ends with a sketch of the Therapeutae.

I. *The Essenes described by Philo, Josephus and Pliny the Elder*

1. *Size and location*

Both Philo and Josephus (in *Ant.*) assert that the membership of the Essene sect exceeded four thousand.[12] It is possible, however, that Josephus borrowed this piece of information from Philo in which case he does not enjoy the status of an independent witness.[13]

---

[6] Note however that the endings *-aios/-enos* are used indiscriminately in Hellenistic Greek.
[7] Cf. PBJS 19–29. Cf. J. J. Bellermann, *Geschichtliche Nachrichten aus dem Alterthume über Essäer und Therapeuten* (1821), 8.
[8] *War* 2. 136.
[9] *Q.o.p.* 75; *V.C.* 2.
[10] PBJS, 24–28; G. Vermes, *Jesus the Jew*, 59–63.
[11] Cf. S. Wagner, *Die Essener in der wissenschaftlichen Discussion* (1960), 114–27.
[12] *Q.o.p.* 75; *Ant.* 18. 21.
[13] Cf. HJP II, 562, n. 1.

Introduction

The Essenes resided in Palestine alone[14] unless Philo's Therapeutae are to be identified with them.[15] They are said to have lived in many towns of Judaea (Philo),[16] or in every town of Palestine (Josephus).[17] On the other hand, Philo claims that they avoided cities because of the immorality of their inhabitants.[18] Pliny's location of the Essenes in the wilderness between Jericho and Engedi must therefore be understood in such a wider context.[19]

2. Communal organization

The local congregations dwelt in commonly occupied houses[20] under the leadership of superiors (*epimeletai*).[21] Full membership was attained in successive stages. Candidates, provided with a white robe, a small hatchet (or rather pick) and an apron, had to undergo a one-year probation before being admitted to Essene ablutions.[22] Then followed a two-year period of initiation,[23] leading, after the swearing of the oath of fidelity, to tablefellowship.[24] Only adult men were received as full members,[25] although boys also are said to have been trained by them.[26]

---

[14] Cf. *Q.o.p.* 75. Josephus (*War* 2.119) simply describes them, together with the Pharisees and the Sadducees, as a Jewish, no doubt Palestinian Jewish, religious party. Pliny locates them in the Judaean desert.
[15] Cf. Appendix below.
[16] *Apol.* 1.
[17] *War* 2. 124.
[18] *Q.o.p.* 75–76.
[19] *Nat. Hist.* 5. 73. On the meaning of *infra hos Engada*, see R. de Vaux, *Archaeology*, 133–7; J.-P. Audet, 'Qumrân et la notice de Pline sur les Esséniens', RB 68 (1961), 346–87; C. Burchard, 'Pline et les Esséniens', RB 69 (1962), 533–69; E. M. Laperroussaz, 'Infra hos Engadda', RB 69 (1962), 369–80. The 1961–65 archaeological excavations in the Engedi area, directed by B. Mazar, found no trace of an Essene settlement 'above' the town. Cf. D. Winton Thomas (ed.), *Archaeology and the Old Testament* (1967), 223–30.
[20] *Apol.* 5; *Q.o.p.* 85; *War* 2. 129.
[21] *War* 2. 134.
[22] *War* 2. 123, 129–31, 137, 148; *V.C.* 66.
[23] *War* 2. 138.
[24] *War* 2. 141.
[25] *Apol.* 3.
[26] *War* 2. 120.

Serious transgression of the rules resulted in expulsion decided by a court of one hundred judges.[27]

3. *Property and work*

New members handed over their property, and subsequently all their earnings to the superiors,[28] and a special official (steward: *tamias*) looked after the members' needs,[29] providing food, clothing, and care for the sick and the elderly, etc.[30] They were permitted to support the needy, but required the procurators' (*epitropoi*) permission in the case of relatives.[31] Travelling brethren were catered for by a special officer or *kedemon*.[32] Their main, though not exclusive, occupation was agriculture.[33] Among strictly forbidden pursuits, Philo singles out commerce and the manufacture of weapons.[34]

4. *Essene moderation and virtuousness*

Both Josephus and Philo extol the moral excellence of the sectaries,[35] especially their rejection of pleasures and control of passions.[36] Their diet was monotonous and extremely frugal;[37] also, they wore their clothes and shoes until they fell to pieces.[38]

5. *Peculiar features*

In addition to abstemiousness and simplicity, the following Essene characteristics are listed by Philo and Josephus:

(a) They opted for a rough appearance and consequently abstained from anointing themselves with oil.[39]

---

[27] *War* 2. 143, 145.
[28] *War* 2. 122–3.
[29] *Apol.* 10.
[30] *Apol.* 12–13; *Q.o.p.* 86–87.
[31] *War* 2. 134.
[32] *War* 2. 124–5.
[33] *Ant.* 18. 19; *Q.o.p.* 78.
[34] *Apol.* 8–9; *Q.o.p.* 78.
[35] *Ant.* 18. 19; *Q.o.p.* 88–91.
[36] *War* 2. 120.
[37] *War* 2. 133; *Apol.* 11.
[38] *War* 2. 126.
[39] *War* 2. 123. Cf. J. M. Baumgarten, *Studies in Qumran Law* (1977), 88–97.

Introduction

(b) They always wore white garments.[40]

(c) They took a purificatory bath, modestly girded with an apron, before both their daily meals[41] and after their natural functions.[42]

(d) Excretion, completely avoided on the Sabbath,[43] was surrounded by the following ritual: they dug a hole with their *axinarion* in some remote place and relieved themselves in it, while modestly concealing themselves under their cloak. Finally, the excrement was covered with earth.[44]

(e) Spitting 'into the middle or towards the right' was forbidden.[45]

(f) Philo, Pliny and Josephus, with the exception of a single passage, declare that the Essenes rejected marriage.[46] The two Jewish writers attribute celibacy to misogyny,[47] although Josephus remarks that they did not condemn marriage in principle.[48] He, indeed, mentions a branch of the sect which permitted marriage and sex as long as it was strictly for the propagation of the species.[49]

(g) There were no slaves in the community as they championed freedom.[50]

(h) They rejected oaths as a means of confirming the veracity of a statement.[51]

(i) For reasons of ritual purity, they kept away from the Temple and declined animal sacrifice.[52] However, they sent offerings to Jerusalem and 'sacrificed among themselves'.[53]

(j) The sect's meals, open to initiates only, were prepared by

[40] *War* 2. 123, 137.
[41] *War* 2. 129.
[42] *War* 2. 129, 149.
[43] *War* 2. 147.
[44] *War* 2. 148–9.
[45] *War* 2. 147.
[46] *Apol.* 11. 14–17; *Nat. Hist.* 5. 73; *War* 2. 120–1; *Ant.* 18. 21.
[47] *Apol.* 11. 14–16; *War* 2. 161.
[48] *War* 2. 121.
[49] *War* 2. 160–1.
[50] *Q.o.p.* 79; *Ant.* 18. 21.
[51] *War* 2. 135; *Q.o.p.* 84. According to *Ant.* 15. 371, the Essenes were exempted by Herod from taking the oath of allegiance which he imposed on his Jewish subjects.
[52] *Ant.* 18. 19; *Q.o.p.* 75. For the text of *Ant.* see L. H. Feldman in Loeb.
[53] *Ant.* 18. 19.

priests following special purity rules.[54] They were taken twice daily after the prescribed ablutions and were preceded and followed by a grace, recited by a priest.[55]

6. *Essene religious thought and practice*

(a) Their paramount theological principle was an absolute belief in Fate (i.e. no doubt divine Providence) in preference to human free-will.[56]

(b) They also held in extreme reverence the ancestral laws and the law-giver.[57] The allegorical interpretation of the Torah was, according to Philo, part of their religious worship.[58]

(c) They advocated a most stringent observance of the Sabbath.[59]

(d) They possessed arcane doctrines, recorded in secret books, which were to be disclosed only to initiates.[60] These teachings included, among others, the names of the angels.[61]

(e) One of their favourite subjects was the study of healing powers beneficial to the soul and the body.[62]

(f) They were also convinced that they had the gift of prophecy, and, if Josephus can be trusted, they seldom made a mistake.[63]

(g) Essene individual eschatology envisages, according to Josephus, the soul's survival after death, the just enjoying eternal bliss and the wicked unending torment.[64] There is nowhere reference to bodily resurrection, a concept hardly reconcilable with Josephus' allusion to the slavery of souls imprisoned in bodies during their lifetime.[65]

[54] *Ant.* 18. 22; *War* 2. 143.
[55] *War* 2. 129–32.
[56] *Ant.* 13. 172; 18. 18.
[57] *War* 2. 145, 159; *Q.o.p.* 80.
[58] *Q.o.p.* 82.
[59] *War* 2. 147; *Q.o.p.* 81.
[60] *War* 2. 142.
[61] *War* 2. 142.
[62] *War* 2. 136.
[63] *War* 2. 159. On Essene prophets mentioned by Josephus, see below.
[64] *War* 2. 154–7.
[65] *War* 2. 154–5. According to Hippolytus (*Ref.* 9.27), Essene beliefs included articles on resurrection, the last judgement and the final conflagration of the universe.

II. The Community of the Dead Sea Scrolls

1. Organization of the Qumran Community[66]

The organization, government and life of the sect can be reconstructed through judicious use of the various codes: 1QS, CD, 1QM/4QM, 1QSa and 11QTS. To succeed in the enterprise, one must bear in mind that 1QS appears to address a 'monastic' group; that CD envisages town communities and camps with members leading ordinary lives; that the Temple Scroll may be originally a pre-Qumran document;[67] that the various sources may testify to customs and laws of successive periods; and that 1QSa and 1/4QM at least partly legislate for the future.

The Qumran *yaḥad* or community modelled itself on the historical Israel, divided into priests and Levites on the one hand, and Israelites on the other (1QS 8:5-9). It was symbolically grouped in twelve tribes (1QM 2:1-3) and each tribe consisted of units of thousands, hundreds, fifties and tens (1QS 2:21-22). Ultimate authority lay in the hands of the priests, designated 'sons of Zadok' or 'sons of Aaron'. Decisions concerning doctrine, justice and property were made by them (1QS 5:2; 9:7), in consultation with the members of their council. Even the smallest unit of ten men, required the presence of a priest to recite grace over the meals (1QS 6:2-5; CD 12:2-3) and to perform functions reserved by the Torah for the sacerdotal class (CD 13:4-7). The priest was also probably the person in charge of Bible study (1QS 6:6).[68]

The leader of the group was known as the *mebaqqer*[69] (overseer, guardian), almost certainly a priest, whose job it was to enquire into the suitability of candidates who wished to join, instruct those undergoing initiation, give rulings and handle practical and financial matters (1QS 6:13-23; CD 13:7-16). The overseer of the work of the congregation (1QS 6:20), if different from the official called simply the *mebaqqer*, may be identified as the community bursar.

[66] For a general outline, see QIP, 87-115; DSSE³, 1-18.
[67] Cf. HJP III.1, 412.
[68] Cf. HJP III.1, 576, n. 6.
[69] Cf. HJP III.1, 576, n. 7.

8   *The Essenes*

The Damascus Document mentions also a priest president and a *mebaqqer* general at the head of the whole organization (CD 14:6–12). Whereas in the Community Rule the council exercises judicial functions, the Damascus Document mentions ten judges elected for a fixed term: four priests and Levites and six Israelites (CD 10:4–10).[70] The various office-holders were subject to a compulsory retiring age: fifty years for the *mebaqqer* of all the camps and sixty for the others (CD 14:7, 9; 10:6–10).

Only eschatological lay leaders are alluded to (apart from the Temple Scroll 57:4–5, 11–12): they are listed from the twelve tribal chiefs down to the chief of ten (1QM 2:1–4; 3:13–4:5; 1QSa 1:29–2:1). The lay head is referred to as the *nasi* or Prince (1QM 5:1; 1QSa 2:14, 20), but the Temple Scroll calls him King (56:13–59:13).

Initiation into the Community as described in 1QS comprised the following stages:

(1) Entry into the Covenant through the swearing of an oath that the candidate would observe the Torah according to the Zadokite priestly interpretation (1QS 1:16–17; 5:1–11; 6:14–15).

(2) Instruction for an unspecified period followed by an examination (1QS 6:15–16).

(3) If accepted, the candidate underwent a first year of special training during which he was not allowed to touch the sect's 'purity' (probably ritually clean solid food as well as the jars, pots and pans reserved for it) or share its goods (1QS 6:16–17).

(4) If he passed the test at the end of the year, he was permitted to touch the 'purity', but not the liquids, and was obliged to transfer his property to the sect's safekeeping, but it was not yet merged with the assets of the community (1QS 6:18–21).

(5) After a final examination at the end of the second year, he was fully integrated, with voting rights and common ownership of goods. The latter entailed the absolute transfer of property and earnings to the financial administrator (1QS 6:21–23). Members were forbidden to receive anything from outsiders except against payment (1QS 5:16–17).

The common life entailed nightly study and prayer meetings (1QS 6:7); the partaking of bread and *tirosh* (wine or unfermented

[70] Cf. J. M. Baumgarten, *Studies in Qumran Law* (1977), 145–71.

grape-juice)[71] at solemn meals blessed by the presiding priest (1QS 6:4-5; 1QSa 2:17-21); and attendance at a yearly general assembly, probably at the Feast of the Renewal of the Covenant, where a review of the sectaries' ranking took place (1QS 1-3; 2:19).

The initiation of new members is given a less detailed account in CD. Outsiders were examined and instructed by the *mebaqqer* (CD 13:11-12), whereas the members' male children, after receiving education and training within the Community (1QSa 1:6-9), made their formal entry at the age of twenty years by swearing the oath of the Covenant (CD 15:5-6). The sect's strict rules applied in the CD group, too, with the exception of those relating to the common ownership of property. Trading with outsiders, even with Gentiles, was permitted (CD 13:14-16; 12:9-11). Charity was financed through a compulsory levy, two day's income per month, administered by the *mebaqqer* and the judges (CD 14:12-16).

Transgression of the biblical Law and of the sectarian rules was punished according to the gravity of each case. Any wilful infringement of the Torah of Moses carried the penalty of irrevocable permanent expulsion (1QS 8:20-24).[72] Likewise a member who turned apostate after ten years in the Community could in no circumstance be readmitted (1QS 7:22-24). Lesser acts of disobedience were punished by temporary (up to two years) exclusion from the common life and by various lesser penances (1QS 6:24-7:21). CD alludes to imprisonment (12:4-6) and to the death penalty (9:1[73]; 12:2-3), as does also the Temple Scroll in connection with treason (67:6-13).[74] The question of marriage and celibacy (temporary or permanent) requires careful consideration of the literary and archaeological data. The Damascus Document, the Temple Scroll, the Messianic Rule (1QSa) and the War Rule mention married members and their children.

---

[71] Cf. QIP, 111.

[72] Cf. G. Forkman, *The Limits of the Religious Community. Expulsion from the Religious Community within the Qumran Sect, within Rabbinic Judaism and within Primitive Christianity* (1972).

[73] Cf. P. Winter, 'Sadoqite Fragment IX, 1', RQ 6 (1967), 131-6; Z. W. Falk, '*Behuqei hagoyim* in Damascus Document IX,1', *ibid.* (1969), 569.

[74] Cf. M. Hengel, *Crucifixion* (1977), 84-5; J. M. Baumgarten, *Studies in Qumran Law* (1977), 172-82.

However, the War Rule stipulates that during the long eschatological conflict no woman or youth should enter the camp of the Sons of Light (1QM 7:4–5). By contrast, the precepts of the Community Rule never refer to female members, a fact that would be inexplicable if there had been women among the sectaries. Issues concerning marriage, divorce, ritual impurity associated with sex, and the education of children, could not have been left undetermined. Hence this is not an ordinary *argumentum e silentio* and it is legitimate to conclude that absence of reference means that there was no problem to address. Similarly, from the archaeological point of view, although female and child skeletons were found in the Qumran cemetery, they are small in number and located on the peripheries of the main graveyard. The latter seems to contain exclusively male remains in numbers totally disproportionate to those of the women and children. It is consequently not the cemetery of an ordinary Jewish settlement.[75]

2. *Qumran religious thought and practice*

The Qumran Community claimed to be founded on a 'new Covenant' (cf. 1QpHab 2:3; CD 8:21, 35), based on the Torah of Moses and the teaching of the prophets and interpreted according to the revelations received by the Teacher of Righteousness and the authoritative exegesis of the Zadokite priestly leaders of the sect.[76]

Each member believed in his special election, through which he received revealed knowledge and divine grace. These heavenly gifts were to lead to holiness, to a continuous life of worship on

---

[75] On celibacy, see A. Marx, 'Les racines du célibat essénien', RQ 70 (1970), 323–42; A. Guillaumont, 'A propos du célibat des Esséniens', *Hommages à A. Dupont-Sommer* (1971), 395–404; J. Coppens, 'Le célibat essénien', *Qumrân*, ed. M. Delcor (1978), 295–303. For Qumran marriage laws, see HJP II, p. 578, n. 14.

[76] Cf. G. Vermes, STJ, 26–66; 96–125; PBJS, 37–49; L. H. Schiffman, *Halakhah at Qumran* (1975); *Sectarian Law in the Dead Sea Scrolls* (1983); J. M. Baumgarten, *Studies in Qumran Law* (1977); H. Gabrion, 'L'interprétation de l'Ecriture dans la littérature de Qumrân', ANRW 19.1 (1979), 779–848; D. Dimant, 'Qumran Sectarian Literature: Biblical Interpretation', JWSTP II.2 (1984), 503–13; HJP III.1, 420–51.

earth linked to the heavenly liturgy performed by the angels in heaven and to the contemplation of divine mysteries, including the vision of the *Merkabah*, God's Throne-Chariot.[77]

Harmony between heavenly and earthly worship required that the sect's liturgies be enacted at the precise times determined by eternal decrees. Hence paramount importance was attached to the recitation at the correct moments of the daily and weekly prayers and the strict observance of seasonal feasts, determined according to the Community's solar calendar.[78]

The biblical laws relating to ritual purity were given a rigorous interpretation, with numerous references to ablutions. A 'baptism' of this kind appears to be associated with the entry into the Covenant.[79] The sect's attitude to the Temple of Jerusalem is not altogether clear. The Temple Scroll legislates on cultic matters *qua* every day realities, and so does the Damascus Document (11:19–20). However, the Qumran priestly view regarding the Sanctuary was that it was a place of pollution where unlawful worship was offered following an invalid calendar. Hence the sect's prayers and holy life were to replace the Jerusalem rituals until the expected restoration of the proper cult in the seventh year of the forty-year eschatological war.[80]

The Community's solemn meal (1QS 6:4–5) counted no doubt as a substitute for the sacrificial meals in the Temple. It was to continue until after the onset of the messianic age (1QSa 2:17–22). At least two, and possibly three, messianic figures were expected: 'the Prophet and the Messiahs of Aaron and Israel' (1QS 9:11); 'the Priest' and 'the Messiah of Israel' (1QSa 2:11–22); 'the Priest' and 'the Prince of the Congregation' (1QSb 5:20–28); 'the Branch of David' and 'the Interpreter of the Law'

---

[77] Cf. QIP, 163–97.

[78] Cf. HJP I, 599–601; II, 581.

[79] Cf. CD 10: 10–13; 1QM 14: 2–3; 1QS 3: 4–5; 5:13. See J. A. Fitzmyer, *Essays on the Semitic Background of the NT* (1971), 469–73; J. Neusner, *The Idea of Purity in Ancient Judaism* (1973).

[80] Cf. G. Vermes, QIP, 180–1, 193; STJ, 26–39; B. Gärtner, *The Temple and the Community in Qumran and the New Testament* (1965); G. Klinzing, *Die Umdeutung des Kultus in der Qumrangemeinde und im N.T.* (1971); J. M. Baumgarten, *Studies in Qumran Law* (1977), 39–56; J. Neusner, *Early Rabbinic Judaism* (1975), 34–49.

(CD 7:18–20; 4QFlor. 1:11).[81] Belief in a spiritual afterlife is well-attested (1QS 11:5–9; 1QH 11:10–14, etc.), but it is uncertain whether it had any clear association with the doctrine of bodily resurrection (cf. 1QH 6:34–35; 11:10–14 where the phrases may be metaphors).[82]

III. The Relationship between the Essenes and the Qumran Sect

There is general scholarly agreement, though not unanimity, in identifying Essenism and Qumran.[83] This agreement is based on the following considerations:

(1) There is no better site than Qumran to correspond to Pliny's Essene settlement between Jericho and Engedi.[84]

(2) The organization, communal life, doctrines and customs portrayed in the relevant sources manifest such fundamental similarities that the identification of the two institutions commands a high degree of probability, provided that the differences between the two descriptions can be explained.[85]

(3) As will be shown presently, the Essenes and the Qumran community existed in an identical chronological setting. Josephus places the Essenes between Jonathan Maccabaeus and the first

---

[81] On the meals, see K. G. Kuhn, 'The Lord's Supper and the Communal Meal at Qumran', *The Scrolls and the NT*, ed. K. Stendahl (1958), 65–93; M. Delcor, 'Repas cultuels esséniens et thérapeutes', RQ 6 (1969), 401–25; J. A. Fitzmyer, *Essays on the Semitic Background of the NT* (1971), 473–5. For messianism, cf. HJP II, 550–4; A. S. van der Woude, *Die messianischen Vorstellungen der Gemeinde von Qumrân* (1957); J. Starcky, 'Les quatre étapes du messianisme à Qumrân', RB 70 (1963), 481–505; A. Caquot, 'Le messianisme qumrânien', *Qumrân*, ed. M. Delcor (1978), 231–47.

[82] Cf. J. van der Ploeg, 'The Belief in Immortality in the Writings of Qumran', Bibliotheca Orientalis 18 (1961), 136–42; G. W. E. Nickelsburg, *Resurrection, Immortality and Eternal Life in Intertestamental Judaism* (1972).

[83] E. L. Sukenik, *Megillot genuzot* I (1948), 16, was the first to propose the Essene theory, followed by A. Dupont-Sommer, *Aperçus préliminaires sur les manuscrits de la Mer Morte* (1950), 105–17; *The Essene Writings from Qumran* (1961), *passim*. Cf. QIP, 125–30, 133–6. The most detailed recent criticism of the Essene identification comes from N. Golb, 'The Problem of Origin and Identification of the Dead Sea Scrolls', Proceedings of the American Philosophical Society 124/1 (1980), 1–24.

[84] Cf. R. de Vaux, *Archaeology and the Dead Sea Scrolls* (1973), 133–8.

[85] Cf. QIP, 127–30.

Jewish rebellion (A.D. 66–70) and archaeologists have assigned the sectarian occupation of Qumran to roughly the same epoch.[86]

Some of the contradictions are attributable to internal lack of uniformity in the sources. Qumran testifies both to common and individual ownership of property; the classical sources emphasize Essene celibacy, but Josephus speaks also of married sectaries; a number of Scrolls mention women and children but 1QS is significantly silent on the subject; at Qumran the swearing of an oath was the first act in the initiation process; according to Josephus, it constituted its climax.

Many of the differences may be due to the diverse nature of the sources. Thus the Qumran texts were written by, and addressed to, members of an esoteric sect, whereas none of the classical witnesses were Essene initiates, not even Josephus.[87] Philo, Pliny and Josephus addressing essentially a non-Jewish readership, modelled their picture of the Essenes to some extent on Hellenistic associations such as the Pythagoraean fellowship (*Ant.* 15. 371). If, in addition, it is borne in mind that the Qumran movement itself incorporated two distinct branches and that its two-hundred years' history necessarily entailed organizational and doctrinal evolutionary changes,[88] and that none of the other identifications with Pharisees, Sadducees, Zealots, or Jewish-Christians commends itself, the theory identifying the Essenes with the 'monastic' brotherhood of Qumran has strong claims for general acceptance.[89]

---

[86] *Ant.* 13. 171; *War* 2. 152, 567. R. de Vaux, *op. cit.*, 5–6.

[87] Josephus claims to have received some Essene training (*Life*, 10), but not a full initiation requiring three years.

[88] According to their prospective editors, the unpublished fragments of 'Some of the Precepts of the Torah' (4QMMT), a polemical work from Cave 4, may reflect the earliest stages of sectarian halakhah. Cf. E. Qimron and J. Strugnell, 'An Unpublished Halakhic Letter from Qumran', in *Biblical Archaeology Today* (1985), 400–7.

[89] For the various non-Essene identifications, see HJP II, 585. For more recent theories associating Qumran with early Christianity, see B. E. Thiering, *Redating the Teacher of Righteousness* (1979); *The Gospels and Qumran: A New Hypothesis* (1981); *The Qumran Origins of the Christian Church* (1983); R. Eisenman, *Maccabees, Zadokites, Christians and Qumran* (1983); *James the Just and the Habakkuk Pesher* (1986). According to N. Golb (*art. cit.* in n. 83, 11, 24), the Dead Sea Scrolls do not represent a single sect, but the literary treasures of various Jerusalem groups, hidden in the Qumran caves during the first war against Rome.

IV. Essene and Qumran History

The classical sources provide but scarce historical information about the Essenes. Philo is completely silent, and Pliny merely implies that the sect existed since time immemorial ('per saeculorum millia ... gens aeterna est'). Josephus furnishes incidental data. He first mentions the Essenes, together with the Pharisees and Sadducees, at the time of Jonathan Maccabaeus in mid-second century B.C. (*Ant.* 13. 171). Next, he alludes to them during the reign of Herod in connection with the exemption granted to the sectaries from the oath of allegiance imposed by this king on his Jewish subjects (*Ant.* 15. 371). His last historical reference to the group as such occurs apropos of their courageous endurance of torture and martyrdom inflicted on them by the Romans during the war (*War* 2. 152-3). Finally, four Essene individuals are named by Josephus: Judas under Aristobulus I (104-3 B.C.), and Menahem, a contemporary of Herod the Great, are described as prophets (*Ant.* 13. 311-13; 15. 373-8), and Simon, flourishing at the time of the ethnarch Archelaus (4 B.C.-A.D. 6), is presented as a dream interpreter (*Ant.* 17. 345-8). In a totally different context, John the Essene appears as the revolutionary commander of the district of Thamna (*War* 2. 567) who was killed at the battle of Ascalon in the early stages of the rebellion (*War* 3. 11, 19).

These data are perfectly compatible with the archaeological and literary information obtained from the Qumran discoveries. According to the quasi universally held opinion, the sectarian establishment is to be placed chronologically between roughly 140-130 B.C. and the first Jewish revolution, A.D. 68 being singled out as the likely *terminus ad quem*.[90] The proposed decipherment of the many cryptic historical allusions in the Dead Sea Scrolls also points to events and persons situated in the second-first centuries B.C. and the first century A.D.[91] Combined, the two sets of evidence may lead to a solid historical hypothesis and synthesis.

---

[90] Cf. in particular, R. de Vaux, *Archaeology and the Dead Sea Scrolls* (1973).
[91] For a detailed discussion of the historical issues, see HJP II, 585-90; QIP 137-62. The individual writers who are opposed to the Essene theory, *ipso facto* declare the Qumran evidence irrelevant to the historical study of Essenism.

Appendix

1. The Therapeutae

In his treatise, *De vita contemplativa*, Philo depicts a community of Jewish contemplatives, designated as Therapeutae, whom he compares with the active Essenes.

Dedicated to self-healing and philosophy (*V.C.* 2, 10–11), they resided in various places in Egypt, especially in the solitude surrounding the Mareotic Lake in the vicinity of Alexandria (21–23). The establishment consisted of communal buildings for worship and meals (32, 36), and private dwellings containing a 'sanctuary' or *monasterion* for study and meditation (25).

There were men and women Therapeutae, but they all lived in celibacy (2, 68). Even in the common sanctuary, they occupied separate enclosures where they could hear, but not not see, each other (32–33).

Those who wished to join the community handed over their belongings to their relations (13). They possessed only one garment for the summer and one for the winter (38), and a white robe for festivals (66). No programme of initiation is mentioned, but an order of seniority existed (30, 67). The leader was referred to as 'the senior member' or 'the president' (31, 79). The younger Therapeutae attended their elders (75).

They prayed daily at dawn, turning towards the rising sun (27, 89), and at sunset (27, 89), and spent the intervening hours in spiritual exercises (28), Bible study (25), accompanied by an allegorical interpretation of Scripture, and the composition of hymns and psalms (28–29). They all aspired to become 'disciples of Moses' (63). They never ate before the evening (34) and always abstained from meat and wine (73–74). Some of them fasted for up to six days (34–35).

During the formal religious service on the Sabbath, which was conducted by the most learned senior member, an allegorical homily was delivered by him (30–32). On the occasion of the 'chief feast' (65), probably the Feast of Weeks, the president pronounced a sermon on a Bible reading (75, 78). Then he sang a hymn, followed by each member present, one after another (80). After the banquet of leavened bread (81) and no wine (74), further songs were sung until sunrise (83–89).

16   *The Essenes*

Thus the Therapeutae sought to become citizens of heaven and of the world (90).

2. *The Therapeutae and the Essenes*

Parallels between the Therapeutae of Philo and the picture of the Essenes are furnished by both Philo and Josephus on the following points:

    (1) communal meals (*Q.o.p.* 86; *War* 128-32–*V.C.* 81);
    (2) celibacy (*Apol.* 14-17; *War* 121; *Ant.* 18.21–*V.C.* 68);
    (3) frugality (Q.o.p. 77; *Apol.* 11; *War* 130, 133–*V.C.* 37);
    (4) extreme reverence for the Torah (*Q.o.p.* 88; *War* 145–*V.C.* 63-64);
    (5) the name [Essenes = Therapeutae?].

Further features common to the Therapeutae and the Essenes noted by Philo only are:

    (6) avoidance of cities (*Q.o.p* 76–*V.C.* 19-20);
    (7) allegorical Bible exegesis (*Q.o.p.* 82–*V.C.* 28);
    (8) summer and winter garments (*Apol.* 12–*V.C.* 38).

Features common to the Therapeutae and the Essenes mentioned by Josephus only are:

    (9) the white robe (*War* 131–*V.C.* 66);
    (10) morning prayer towards the sun (*War* 128–*V.C.* 27, 89);
    (11) the presence of youth among them (*War* 120–*V.C.* 67-68);
    (12) sectarian literature (*War* 142–*V.C.* 29);
    (13) the practice of healing (*War* 136–*V.C.* 2);
    (14) prophetic gifts (*War* 129–*V.C.* 26);
    (15) self-defence against robbers (*War* 125–*V.C.* 24).

By contrast, there are a number of points where parallels are either lacking, or where there even seems to be a contradiction between Therapeutae and Essenes. These are:

    (a) vegetarianism and abstinence from wine;
    (b) the chief feast;
    (c) the geographical location;
    (d) the number of daily meals;
    (e) male and female celibates;
    (f) contemplative/active life;
    (g) common ownership of property.

The geographical factor is not conclusive because Philo once

implies that the Therapeutae were found 'in many places of the universe' (21), and the problem concerning property ownership may be of Philo's own making. In fact, he simply by-passes the whole issue of the economic regime. The other features, some of them more significant than others, need to be weighed up with care in an attempt to determine the precise relation between Therapeutae and Essenes.

3. *The Therapeutae and the Qumran Community*

Among the most important common characteristics may be noted the fact that at the festal vigil individual Therapeutae sang hymns one after the other, and at the Qumran messianic banquet separate benedictions were recited by each participant (1QSa 2:17–21). Likewise, the Theraputae were expressly instructed to gesticulate with the right hand alone (77), whereas the Qumran sectaries were explicitly forbidden to use their left hand for the same purpose (1QS 7:15). Last but not least, both Therapeutae and Qumran adopted a Pentecontade calendar.[92] The principal difficulty concerns the abstinence from meat and wine among the Therapeutae, while the Qumran sectaries drank *tirosh*, which may have been wine,[93] and may have eaten meat, according to the findings of the archaeologists.[94]

All in all, the available evidence does not justify a complete identification of the Therapeutae and the Essenes/Qumran sectaries. The most likely conclusion is that the former represented an Egyptian off-shoot of the Palestinian ascetic movement of the Essenes.[95]

---

[92] Cf. HJP I, 600, n. 31; J. M. Baumgarten, *Studies in Qumran Law* (1977), 131–42; Y. Yadin, *The Temple Scroll* I (1983), 116–19.
[93] Cf. above, n. 71.
[94] Cf. R. de Vaux, *Archaeology and the Dead Sea Scrolls* (1973), 12–13, 111.
[95] Cf. HJP II, 595–7 and the literature given on p. 597, n. 20.

THE SOURCES

1. Philo

Philo Judaeus (*c.* 30 B.C.–A.D. 45) was a leading figure in the Jewish community of Alexandria, which he represented on the embassy sent to Rome in A.D. 39–40 to request that Jews be exempted from worshipping the emperor Gaius Caligula. Much of his voluminous work survives, largely as a result of later Christian enthusiasm for his ideas. Philo attempted to demonstrate a substantial similarity between Greek philosophy and Jewish doctrines by using allegory to interpret biblical law and narrative. His main Greek sources were Plato, Aristotle, the Stoics and to some extent Neopythagoreanism. It is debated whether his ideas about Judaism were derived from a separate Alexandrian Jewish school or from a common pool of Jewish exegesis and midrash also found in Palestine. It is not certain whether Philo ever visited Judaea or knew Hebrew, but it is in general likely that, whatever accurate information he had about the Essenes, he will have interpreted it to make moral points to his audience of Greek Jews and gentiles, and to point up similarities between the Essenes and Greek philosophical trends.

(a) Philo, *Quod omnis probus liber sit* 75–91

Q.o.p.—'That every good man is free'—is really only the second half of a larger work which considered in its lost first half how a wicked man is by definition a slave. This section of the work was reproduced by Eusebius in *Praep. ev.* viii 12. The authenticity of the ascription of the treatise to Philo has been questioned but is now generally accepted. The work is much influenced by Stoicism and there are many allusions to Greek literature; by contrast, there is little reference to Scripture. It is particularly likely that in this context Philo may have produced an over-idealised view of the Essenes.

20   The Essenes

75 Ἔστι δὲ καὶ ἡ Παλαιστίνη Συρία καλοκἀγαθίας οὐκ ἄγονος, ἣν
πολυανθρωποτάτου ἔθνους τῶν Ἰουδαίων οὐκ ὀλίγη μοῖρα νέμεται.
λέγονταί τινες παρ' αὐτοῖς ὄνομα Ἐσσαῖοι, πλῆθος ὑπερ-
τετρακισχίλιοι, κατ' ἐμὴν δόξαν—οὐκ ἀκριβεῖ τύπῳ διαλέκτου
Ἑλληνικῆς—παρώνυμοι ὁσιότητος, ἐπειδὴ κἂν τοῖς μάλιστα θεραπευταὶ θεοῦ γεγόνασιν, οὐ ζῷα καταθύοντες, ἀλλ' ἱεροπρεπεῖς
76 τὰς ἑαυτῶν διανοίας κατασκευάζειν ἀξιοῦντες. οὗτοι τὸ μὲν
πρῶτον κωμηδὸν οἰκοῦσι τὰς πόλεις ἐκτρεπόμενοι διὰ τὰς τῶν
πολιτευομένων χειροήθεις ἀνομίας, εἰδότες ἐκ τῶν συνόντων ὡς
ἀπ' ἀέρος φθοροποιοῦ νόσον ἐγγινομένην προσβολὴν ψυχαῖς
ἀνίατον· ὧν οἱ μὲν γεωπονοῦντες, οἱ δὲ τέχνας μετιόντες ὅσαι
συνεργάτιδες εἰρήνης, ἑαυτούς τε καὶ τοὺς πλησιάζοντας ὠφελ-
οῦσιν, οὐκ ἄργυρον καὶ χρυσὸν θησαυροφυλακοῦντες οὐδ' ἀποτομὰς
γῆς μεγάλας κτώμενοι δι' ἐπιθυμίαν προσόδων, ἀλλ' ὅσα πρὸς τὰς
77 ἀναγκαίας τοῦ βίου χρείας ἐκπορίζοντες. μόνοι γὰρ ἐξ ἁπάντων
σχεδὸν ἀνθρώπων ἀχρήματοι καὶ ἀκτήμονες γεγονότες ἐπιτηδεύ-
σει τὸ πλέον ἢ ἐνδείᾳ εὐτυχίας πλουσιώτατοι νομίζονται, τὴν
78 ὀλιγοδεΐαν καὶ εὐκολίαν, ὅπερ ἐστί, κρίνοντες περιουσίαν. βελῶν ἢ
ἀκόντων ἢ ξιφιδίων ἢ κράνους ἢ θώρακος ἢ ἀσπίδος οὐδένα παρ'
αὐτοῖς ἂν εὕροις δημιουργὸν οὐδὲ συνόλως ὁπλοποιὸν ἢ μηχανο-
ποιὸν ἤ τι τῶν κατὰ πόλεμον ἐπιτηδεύοντα· ἀλλ' οὐδὲ ὅσα τῶν
κατ' εἰρήνην εὐόλισθα εἰς κακίαν· ἐμπορίας γὰρ ἢ καπηλείας ἢ
ναυκληρίας οὐδ' ὄναρ ἴσασι, τὰς εἰς πλεονεξίαν ἀφορμὰς
79 ἀποδιοπομπούμενοι. δοῦλός τε παρ' αὐτοῖς οὐδὲ εἷς ἐστιν, ἀλλ'
ἐλεύθεροι πάντες ἀνθυπουργοῦντες ἀλλήλοις· καταγινώσκουσί τε
τῶν δεσποτῶν, οὐ μόνον ὡς ἀδίκων, ἰσότητα λυμαινομένων, ἀλλὰ
καὶ ὡς ἀσεβῶν, θεσμὸν φύσεως ἀναιρούντων, ἣ πάντας ὁμοίως
γεννήσασα καὶ θρεψαμένη μητρὸς δίκην ἀδελφοὺς γνησίους, οὐ
λεγομένους ἀλλ' ὄντας ὄντως, ἀπειργάσατο· ὧν τὴν συγγένειαν ἡ
ἐπίβουλος πλεονεξία παρευημερήσασα διέσεισεν, ἀντ' οἰκειότητος
80 ἀλλοτριότητα καὶ ἀντὶ φιλίας ἔχθραν ἐργασαμένη. φιλοσοφίας τε
τὸ μὲν λογικὸν ὡς οὐκ ἀναγκαῖον εἰς κτῆσιν ἀρετῆς λογοθήραις, τὸ
δὲ φυσικὸν ὡς μεῖζον ἢ κατὰ ἀνθρωπίνην φύσιν μετεωρολέσχαις
ἀπολιπόντες, πλὴν ὅσον αὐτοῦ περὶ ὑπάρξεως θεοῦ καὶ τῆς τοῦ

---

[1] This locates Essenes in Palestine, but does it imply that they *only* live there? Cf. *V.C.* 22.
[2] For the number, cf. *Ant.* 18. 20.
[3] For this spelling, see *Ant.* 15. 371; 17. 346; *War* 1. 78;2. 113, 567; 3. 11.
[4] A pun in Greek, see below, sect. 91; *Apol.* 1.

Nor is Palestinian Syria, which is occupied by a considerable part of the very populous nation of the Jews, barren of virtue.[1] Certain among them, to the number of over four thousand,[2] are called Essaeans;[3] although this word is not, strictly speaking, Greek, I think it may be related to the word 'holiness'.[4] Indeed, they are men utterly dedicated to the service of God; they do not offer animal sacrifice, judging it more fitting to render their minds truly holy.[5] First it should be explained that, fleeing the cities because of the ungodliness customary among town-dwellers, they live in villages;[6] for they know that, as noxious air breeds epidemics there, so does the social life afflict the soul with incurable ills. Some Essaeans work in the fields, and others practise various crafts contributing to peace; and in this way they are useful to themselves and to their neighbours. They do not hoard silver and gold, and do not acquire vast domains with the intention of drawing revenue from them, but they procure for themselves only what is necessary to life. Almost alone among all mankind, they live without goods and without property; and this by preference, and not as a result of a reverse of fortune. They think themselves thus very rich, rightly considering frugality and contentment to be real superabundance. In vain would one look among them for makers of arrows, or javelins, or swords, or helmets, or armour, or shields; in short, for makers of arms, or military machines, or any instrument of war, or even of peaceful objects which might be turned to evil purpose. They have not the smallest idea, not even a dream, of wholesale, retail, or marine commerce, rejecting everything that might excite them to cupidity.[7] There are no slaves among them, not a single one, but being all free they help one another.[8] And they condemn slave-owners, not only as unjust in that they offend against equality, but still more as ungodly, in that they transgress the law of nature which, having given birth to all men equally and nourished them like a mother, makes of them true brothers, not in name but in reality. But for its own greater enjoyment crafty avarice has dealt mortal blows at this human kinship, putting hostility in the place of affection, and hatred in the place of friendship. As regards philosophy, they first of all leave logic to word-chasers, seeing that it is useless in the acquisition of virtue; then they leave natural philosophy to street

---

[5] On sacrifices, contrast *Ant.* 18.19; IQM 2 and Temple Scroll.

[6] On avoiding towns, contrast *Apol.* 1; *War* 2. 124.

[7] Cf. *Apol.* 8–9; *Ant.* 18.19, re agriculture. Contrast IQS 5: 16–17; CD 12: 8–10; 13: 14–15.

[8] Slaves: cf. *Ant.* 18.21; but see also CD 12:11

παντὸς γενέσεως φιλοσοφεῖται, τὸ ἠθικὸν εὖ μάλα διαπονοῦσιν ἀλείπταις χρώμενοι τοῖς πατρίοις νόμοις, οὓς ἀμήχανον ἀνθρωπίνην ἐπινοῆσαι ψυχὴν ἄνευ κατοκωχῆς ἐνθέου. τούτους ἀναδιδάσκονται μὲν καὶ παρὰ τὸν ἄλλον χρόνον, ἐν δὲ ταῖς ἑβδόμαις διαφερόντως. ἱερὰ γὰρ ἡ ἑβδόμη νενόμισται, καθ' ἣν τῶν ἄλλων ἀνέχοντες ἔργων, εἰς ἱεροὺς ἀφικνούμενοι τόπους, οἳ καλοῦνται συναγωγαί, καθ' ἡλικίας ἐν τάξεσιν ὑπὸ πρεσβυτέροις νέοι καθέζονται, μετὰ κόσμου τοῦ προσήκοντος ἔχοντες ἀκροατικῶς. εἶθ' εἷς μέν τις τὰς βίβλους ἀναγινώσκει λαβών, ἕτερος δὲ τῶν ἐμπειροτάτων ὅσα μὴ γνώριμα παρελθὼν ἀναδιδάσκει· τὰ γὰρ πλεῖστα διὰ συμβόλων ἀρχαιοτρόπῳ ζηλώσει παρ' αὐτοῖς φιλοσοφεῖται. παιδεύονται δὲ εὐσέβειαν, ὁσιότητα, δικαιοσύνην, οἰκονομίαν, πολιτείαν, ἐπιστήμην τῶν πρὸς ἀλήθειαν ἀγαθῶν καὶ κακῶν καὶ ἀδιαφόρων, αἱρέσεις ὧν χρὴ καὶ φυγὰς τῶν ἐναντίων, ὅροις καὶ κανόσι τριττοῖς χρώμενοι, τῷ τε φιλοθέῳ καὶ φιλαρέτῳ καὶ φιλανθρώπῳ. τοῦ μὲν οὖν φιλοθέου δείγματα παρέχονται μυρία· τὴν παρ' ὅλον τὸν βίον συνεχῆ καὶ ἐπάλληλον ἁγνείαν, τὸ ἀνώμοτον, τὸ ἀψευδές, τὸ πάντων μὲν ἀγαθῶν αἴτιον, κακοῦ δὲ μηδενὸς νομίζειν εἶναι τὸ θεῖον· τοῦ δὲ φιλαρέτου τὸ ἀφιλοχρήματον, τὸ ἀφιλόδοξον, τὸ ἀφιλήδονον, τὸ ἐγκρατές, τὸ καρτερικόν, ἔτι δὲ ὀλιγοδεΐαν, ἀφέλειαν, εὐκολίαν, τὸ ἄτυφον, τὸ νόμιμον, τὸ εὐσταθές, καὶ ὅσα τούτοις ὁμοιότροπα· τοῦ δὲ φιλανθρώπου εὔνοιαν, ἰσότητα, τὴν παντὸς λόγου κρείττονα κοινωνίαν, περὶ ἧς οὐκ ἄκαιρον βραχέα εἰπεῖν. πρῶτον μὲν τοίνυν οὐδενὸς οἰκία τίς ἐστιν ἰδία, ἣν οὐχὶ πάντων εἶναι κοινὴν συμβέβηκε· πρὸς γὰρ τῷ κατὰ θιάσους συνοικεῖν ἀναπέπταται καὶ τοῖς ἑτέρωθεν ἀφικνουμένοις τῶν ὁμοζήλων. εἶτ' ἐστὶ ταμεῖον ἓν πάντων καὶ δαπάναι ⟨κοιναί⟩, καὶ κοιναὶ μὲν ἐσθῆτες, κοιναὶ δὲ τροφαὶ συσσίτια πεποιημένων· τὸ γὰρ ὁμωρόφιον ἢ ὁμοδίαιτον ἢ ὁμοτράπεζον οὐκ ἄν τις εὕροι παρ' ἑτέροις μᾶλλον ἔργῳ βεβαιούμενον· καὶ μήποτ' εἰκότως· ὅσα γὰρ ἂν μεθ' ἡμέραν ἐργασάμενοι λάβωσιν ἐπὶ μισθῷ, ταῦτ' οὐκ ἴδια φυλάττουσιν, ἀλλ' εἰς μέσον

---

[9] Cf. *War* 2. 159.
[10] Shabbat: cf. *War* 2. 147; CD 10:14–11:18.
[11] See the list of virtues in *War* 2. 139 and cf. 1QS 5: 7 f.; CD 15: 5 f.; 1QH 14: 17 f.

orators, seeing that it is beyond human nature, except, however, in what it teaches of the existence of God and the origin of the world. But they work at ethics with extreme care, constantly utilizing the ancestral laws, laws which no human mind could have conceived without divine inspiration.[9] They continually instruct themselves in these laws but especially every seventh day; for the seventh day is thought holy.[10] On that day they abstain from other work and proceed to the holy places called synagogues, where they sit in appointed places, according to their age, the young men below the old, attentive and well-behaved. One of them then takes up the books and reads, and another from among the more learned steps forward and explains whatever is not easy to understand in these books. Most of the time, and in accordance with an ancient method of inquiry, instruction is given them by means of symbols. They learn piety, holiness, justice, the domestic rule, the constitution, knowledge of what is truly good or bad or indifferent, and how to choose what must be done and how to flee from what must be avoided. In this they make use of triple definitions and rules concerning, respectively, the love of God, the love of virtue, and the love of men.[11] Of their love of God they give a thousand examples by constant and unceasing purity throughout the whole of life, by the rejection of oaths,[12] the rejection of falsehood, and by the belief that the Deity is the cause of all good, but of no evil; of their love of virtue, by contempt for riches, glory and pleasure, and by their continence and endurance, and also frugality, simplicity, contentment, modesty, obedience to the rule, stability of character, and all similar virtues; of their love of men, by kindness, equality and a communal life of which, although beyond all praise, it is not out of place to speak briefly here. Firstly, no house belongs to any one man; indeed, there is no house which does not belong to them all, for as well as living in communities, their homes are open to members of the sect arriving from elsewhere.[13] Secondly, there is but one purse for them all and a common expenditure. Their clothes and food are also held in common, for they have adopted the practice of eating together. In vain would one search elsewhere for a more effective sharing of the same roof, the same way of life and the same table.[14] This is the reason: whatever they receive as salary for their day's work is not

---

[12] Cf. *War* 2. 135 and refs. there.
[13] See *Apol.* 5; *War* 2. 129.
[14] On the meal, cf. *V.C.* 36 f., 64, 89; 1QS 6: 4 f.; 1QSa 2: 17–22.

προτιθέντες κοινὴν τοῖς ἐθέλουσι χρῆσθαι τὴν ἀπ' αὐτῶν παρασ-
87 κευάζουσιν ὠφέλειαν. οἵ τε νοσοῦντες οὐχ ὅτι πορίζειν ἀδυ-
νατοῦσιν ἀμελοῦνται, τὰ πρὸς τὰς νοσηλείας ἐκ τῶν κοινῶν
ἔχοντες ἐν ἑτοίμῳ, ὡς μετὰ πάσης ἀδείας ἐξ ἀφθονωτέρων
ἀναλίσκειν. αἰδὼς δ' ἐστὶ πρεσβυτέρων καὶ φροντίς, οἷα γονέων
ὑπὸ γνησίων παίδων χερσὶ καὶ διανοίαις μυρίαις ἐν ἀφθονίᾳ τῇ
88 πάσῃ γηροτροφουμένων. τοιούτους ἡ δίχα περιεργίας Ἑλληνικῶν
ὀνομάτων ἀθλητὰς ἀρετῆς ἀπεργάζεται φιλοσοφία, γυμνάσματα
προτιθεῖσα τὰς ἐπαινετὰς πράξεις, ἐξ ὧν ἡ ἀδούλωτος ἐλευθερία
89 βεβαιοῦται. σημεῖον δέ· πολλῶν κατὰ καιροὺς ἐπαναστάντων τῇ
χώρᾳ δυναστῶν καὶ φύσεσι καὶ προαιρέσεσι χρησαμένων
διαφερούσαις—οἱ μὲν γὰρ πρὸς τὸ ἀτίθασον ἀγριότητα θηρίων
ἐκνικῆσαι σπουδάσαντες, οὐδὲν παραλιπόντες τῶν εἰς ὠμότητα,
τοὺς ὑπηκόους ἀγεληδὸν ἱερεύοντες ἢ καὶ ζῶντας ἔτι μαγείρων
τρόπον κατὰ μέρη καὶ μέλη κρεουργοῦντες ἄχρι τοῦ τὰς αὐτὰς
ὑπομεῖναι συμφορὰς ὑπὸ τῆς τὰ ἀνθρώπεια ἐφορώσης δίκης οὐκ
90 ἐπαύσαντο· οἱ δὲ τὸ παρακεκινημένον καὶ λελυττηκὸς εἰς ἑτέρας
εἶδος κακίας μεθαρμοσάμενοι, πικρίαν ἄλεκτον ἐπιτηδεύσαντες,
ἡσυχῇ διαλαλοῦντες, ἠρεμαιοτέρας φωνῆς ὑποκρίσει βαρύμηνι
ἦθος ἐπιδεικνύμενοι, κυνῶν ἰοβόλων τρόπον προσσαίνοντες,
ἀνιάτων γενόμενοι κακῶν αἴτιοι, κατὰ πόλεις μνημεῖα τῆς ἑαυτῶν
ἀσεβείας καὶ μισανθρωπίας ἀπέλιπον τὰς τῶν πεπονθότων
91 ἀλήστους συμφοράς—, ἀλλὰ γὰρ οὐδεὶς οὔτε τῶν σφόδρα
ὠμοθύμων οὔτε τῶν πάνυ δολερῶν καὶ ὑπούλων ἴσχυσε τὸν
λεχθέντα τῶν Ἐσσαίων ἢ ὁσίων ὅμιλον αἰτιάσασθαι, πάντες δὲ
ἀσθενέστεροι τῆς τῶν ἀνδρῶν καλοκἀγαθίας γενόμενοι καθάπερ
αὐτονόμοις καὶ ἐλευθέροις οὖσιν ἐκ φύσεως προσηνέχθησαν,
ᾄδοντες αὐτῶν τὰ συσσίτια καὶ τὴν παντὸς λόγου κρείττονα
κοινωνίαν, ἣ βίου τελείου καὶ σφόδρα εὐδαίμονός ἐστι σαφέστατον
δεῖγμα.

[15] On common ownership, cf. *Apol.* 4 and refs. there; *War* 2. 122 and refs. there.

kept to themselves, but it is deposited before them all, in their midst, to be put to the common employment of those who wish to make use of it. As for the sick, they are not neglected on the pretext that they can produce nothing, for, thanks to the common purse, they have whatever is needed to treat them, so there is no fear of great expense on their behalf.[15] The aged, for their part, are surrounded with respect and care: they are like parents whose children lend them a helping hand in their old age with perfect generosity and surround them with a thousand attentions.

Such are the athletes of virtue which this philosophy produces, a philosophy which undoubtedly lacks the refinements of Greek eloquence, but which propounds, like gymnastic exercises, the accomplishment of praiseworthy deeds as the means by which a man ensures absolute freedom for himself. And this is the proof. Over the course of time, many kings of diverse character and inclinations have risen against this land. Some, rivalling the most ferocious wild beasts in their cruelty, sparing no sort of atrocity, immolating their subjects in flocks, and even dismembering them alive, piece by piece, limb by limb, like butchers, never ceased until they were themselves obliged to undergo the same misfortunes beneath the blows of that Justice which watches over human destiny. Others, replacing frenzy and rage with another kind of wickedness, nourishing unutterable cruelty, speaking calmly yet revealing beneath their soft-worded hypocrisy a soul filled with profound hatred, caressing as dogs whose bite is poison, these authors of incurable evils left as monuments to their wickedness, from town to town, the never-to-be-forgotten calamities of whose who had suffered. But none of them, neither the most cruel, nor the most unprincipled and false, was ever able to lay a charge against the society known as Essaeans, or Saints;[16] on the contrary, they were all defeated by the virtue of these men. They could only treat them as independent individuals, free by nature, and extol their communal meals and communal life as beyond all praise and as the clearest demonstration of a perfect and completely happy existence.

---

[16] A pun in Greek, cf. sect. 75; *Apol.* 1.

(b) Philo, *Apologia pro Iudaeis* [probably to be identified with the work *Hypothetica* known to have been written by Philo]

Knowledge of this treatise depends almost entirely on the fragments quoted by Eusebius in *Praep. ev.* viii 6-7. The work was clearly intended to defend Jews against unfavourable criticism

1   Μυρίους δὲ τῶν γνωρίμων ὁ ἡμέτερος νομοθέτης ἤλειψεν ἐπὶ κοινωνίαν, οἳ καλοῦνται μὲν Ἐσσαῖοι, παρὰ τὴν ὁσιότητά μοι δοκῶ τῆς προσηγορίας ἀξιωθέντες. οἰκοῦσι δὲ πολλὰς μὲν πόλεις τῆς Ἰουδαίας, πολλὰς δὲ κώμας καὶ μεγάλους καὶ πολυανθρώπους
2   ὁμίλους. ἔστι δ' αὐτοῖς ἡ προαίρεσις οὐ γένει—γένος γὰρ ἐφ' ἑκουσίοις οὐ γράφεται—, διὰ δὲ ζῆλον ἀρετῆς καὶ φιλανθρωπίας
3   ἵμερον. Ἐσσαίων γοῦν κομιδῇ νήπιος οὐδεὶς ἀλλ' οὐδὲ πρωτογένειος ἢ μειράκιον, ἐπεὶ τά γε τούτων ἀβέβαια ἤθη τῷ τῆς ἡλικίας ἀτελεῖ συννεωτερίζονται· τέλειοι δ' ἄνδρες καὶ πρὸς γῆρας ἀποκλίνοντες ἤδη, μηκέθ' ὑπὸ τῆς τοῦ σώματος ἐπιρροῆς κατακλυζόμενοι μηδ' ὑπὸ τῶν παθῶν ἀγόμενοι, τὴν ἀψευδῆ δὲ καὶ μόνην ὄντως ἐλευθερίαν καρπούμενοι. μάρτυς δὲ τῆς ἐλευθερίας αὐτῶν ὁ
4   βίος. ἴδιον οὐδεὶς οὐδὲν ὑπομένει κτήσασθαι τὸ παράπαν, οὐκ οἰκίαν, οὐκ ἀνδράποδον, οὐ χωρίον, οὐ βοσκήματα, οὐχ ὅσα ἄλλα παρασκευαὶ καὶ χορηγίαι πλούτου· πάντα δ' εἰς μέσον ἀθρόα
5   καταθέντες κοινὴν καρποῦνται τὴν ἁπάντων ὠφέλειαν. οἰκοῦσι δ' ἐν ταὐτῷ, κατὰ θιάσους ἑταιρίας καὶ συσσίτια πεποιημένοι, καὶ
6   πάνθ' ὑπὲρ τοῦ κοινωφελοῦς πραγματευόμενοι διατελοῦσιν. ἀλλ' ἑτέρων ἕτεραι πραγματεῖαι, αἷς ἐπαποδύντες ἀόκνως διαθλοῦσιν, οὐ κρυμόν, οὐ θάλπος, οὐχ ὅσα ἀέρος νεωτερίσματα προφασιζόμενοι· πρὶν δ' ἥλιον ἀνασχεῖν ἐπὶ τὰ συνήθη τρεπόμενοι, δυομένου μόλις ἐπανίασι χαίροντες οὐχ ἧττον τῶν ἐν τοῖς γυμνικοῖς
7   ἐξεταζομένων ἀγῶσιν. ὑπολαμβάνουσι γὰρ ἄττ' ἂν ἐπιτηδεύωσιν εἶναι βιωφελέστερα καὶ ἡδίω ψυχῇ καὶ σώματι τὰ γυμνάσματα καὶ πολυχρονιώτερα τῶν ἐν ἀθλήσεσι, μὴ συναφηβῶντα τῇ τοῦ
8   σώματος ἀκμῇ. εἰσὶ γὰρ αὐτῶν οἱ μὲν γεηπόνοι, τῶν περὶ σπορὰν καὶ φυτουργίαν ἐπιστήμονες, οἱ δ' ἀγελάρχαι, παντοδαπῶν θρεμ-
9   μάτων ἡγεμόνες, ἔνιοι δὲ σμήνη μελιττῶν ἐπιτροπεύουσιν. ἄλλοι

---

[1] A pun, cf. *Q.o.p.* 75, 91.
[2] Cf. *War* 2. 124, but contrast *Q.o.p.* 75-6.

by gentiles and had a non-Jewish audience in mind. It is not clear precisely what accusation was being countered by Philo through his description of the Essenes.

Our Law-giver encouraged the multitude of his disciples to live in community: these are called Essaeans, and I think they have merited this title because of their holiness.[1] They live in a number of towns in Judaea,[2] and also in many villages and large groups. Their enlistment is not due to race (the word race is unsuitable where volunteers are concerned), but is due to zeal for the cause of virtue and an ardent love of men. There are therefore no children of tender years among the Essaeans, nor even adolescents or young men, since at this age the character, because of its immaturity, is inconstant and attracted to novelty; but they are men of ripe years already inclining to old age who are no longer carried away by the flux of the body nor drawn by the passions, but enjoy true and unparalleled liberty. Their life bears witness to this liberty. None of them can endure to possess anything of his own; neither house, slave, field, nor flocks, nor anything which feeds and procures wealth. But they set down everything in a heap in their midst, and enjoy in common the resources of them all.[3] They live together in brotherhoods,[4] having adopted the form of associations and the custom of eating in common. They employ their whole activity for the common good. Nevertheless, they all follow different occupations, and apply themselves to them with zeal, like athletes, never offering as excuse either cold, or heat, or atmospheric changes. Performing their accustomed tasks from before sunrise, they do not leave them until the sun has almost set, devoting themselves to them with no less joy than those who train for gymnastic combat. Indeed, they believe their own training to be more useful to life, more agreeable to body and soul, and more lasting, than athletic games, since their exercises remain fitted to their age, even when the body no longer possesses its full strength. There are farmers among them expert in the art of sowing and cultivation of plants, shepherds leading every sort of flock, and bee-keepers. Others are craftsmen in divers trades. So they have to suffer no

1
2
3
4
5
6
7
8
9

[3] Common property: cf. 1QS 1: 11–13; 6: 17, 19 f.; 1Qp Hab. 12: 9 f.
[4] See *Q.o.p.* 85; *War* 2. 129.

δὲ δημιουργοὶ τῶν κατὰ τέχνας εἰσίν, ὑπὲρ τοῦ μηδὲν ὧν αἱ ἀναγκαῖαι χρεῖαι βιάζονται παθεῖν, οὐδὲν ἀναβαλλόμενοι τῶν εἰς πορισμὸν ἀνυπαίτιον. ἐκ δὴ τῶν οὕτως διαφερόντων ἕκαστοι τὸν μισθὸν λαβόντες ἑνὶ διδόασι τῷ χειροτονηθέντι ταμίᾳ· λαβὼν δ' ἐκεῖνος αὐτίκα τἀπιτήδεια ὠνεῖται καὶ παρέχει τροφὰς ἀφθόνους καὶ τἆλλα ὧν ὁ ἀνθρώπινος βίος χρειώδης. οἱ δ' ὁμοδίαιτοι καὶ ὁμοτράπεζοι καθ' ἑκάστην ἡμέραν εἰσὶ τοῖς αὐτοῖς ἀσμενίζοντες, ὀλιγοδείας ἐρασταί, πολυτέλειαν ὡς ψυχῆς καὶ σώματος νόσον ἐκτρεπόμενοι. κοινὴ δ' οὐ τράπεζα μόνον, ἀλλὰ καὶ ἐσθὴς αὐτοῖς ἐστι. πρόκεινται γὰρ χειμῶνι μὲν στιφραὶ χλαῖναι, θέρει δ' ἐξωμίδες εὐτελεῖς, ὡς εὐμαρῶς ἐξεῖναι τῷ βουλομένῳ ἣν ἂν ἐθελήσῃ λαβεῖν, ἐπειδὴ καὶ τὰ ἑνὸς ἁπάντων καὶ τὰ πάντων ἔμπαλιν ἑνὸς ὑπείληπται. καὶ μὴν εἴ τις αὐτῶν ἀσθενήσειεν, ἐκ τῶν κοινῶν νοσηλεύεται, θεραπευόμενος ταῖς ἁπάντων ἐπιμελείαις καὶ φροντίσιν. οἱ δὲ δὴ πρεσβῦται κἂν εἰ τύχοιεν ἄτεκνοι, καθάπερ οὐ πολύπαιδες μόνον, ἀλλὰ καὶ σφόδρα εὔπαιδες, ἐν εὐτυχεστάτῳ καὶ λιπαρωτάτῳ γήρᾳ τὸν βίον εἰώθασι καταλύειν, ὑπὸ τοσούτων προνομίας ἀξιούμενοι καὶ τιμῆς, ἑκουσίῳ γνώμῃ μᾶλλον ἢ φύσεως ἀνάγκῃ θεραπεύειν ἀξιούντων. ἔτι τοίνυν ὅπερ ἢ μόνον ἢ μάλιστα τὴν κοινωνίαν ἔμελλε διαλύειν, ὀξυδερκέστερον ἰδόντες γάμον παρῃτήσαντο μετὰ τοῦ καὶ διαφερόντως ἀσκεῖν ἐγκράτειαν. Ἐσσαίων γὰρ οὐδεὶς ἄγεται γυναῖκα, διότι φίλαυτον γυνὴ καὶ ζηλότυπον οὐ μετρίως καὶ δεινὸν ἀνδρὸς ἤθη παλεῦσαι καὶ συνεχέσι γοητείαις ὑπαγαγέσθαι. μελετήσασα γὰρ θῶπας λόγους καὶ τὴν ἄλλην ὑπόκρισιν, ὥσπερ ἐπὶ σκηνῆς, ὄψεις καὶ ἀκοὰς ὅταν δελεάσῃ, διηπατημένων οἷα ὑπηκόων τὸν ἡγεμόνα νοῦν φενακίζει. παῖδες δ' εἰ γένοιντο, φρονήματος ὑποπλησθεῖσα καὶ παρρησίας, ὅσα κατ' εἰρωνείαν πρότερον ὑπούλως ὑπηνίττετο, ταῦτα ἀπ' εὐτολμοτέρου θράσους ἐκλαλεῖ καὶ ἀναισχυντοῦσα βιάζεται πράττειν, ὧν ἕκαστον κοινωνίας ἐχθρόν. ὁ γὰρ ἢ γυναικὸς φίλτροις ἐνδεθεὶς ἢ τέκνων ἀνάγκῃ φύσεως προκηδόμενος οὐκέτι πρὸς

---

[5] Cf. *Q.o.p.* 78 on forbidden trades.
[6] See *War* 2. 123; 1QS 6: 20, and refs. at *War* 2. 134.
[7] Care of sick and elderly: cf. CD 18: 1–5.

privation of what is indispensable to essential needs, and they never defer until the morrow whatever serves to procure for them blameless revenue.[5] When each man receives his salary for these different trades, he hands it over to one person, the steward elected by them,[6] and as soon as the steward receives this money, he immediately buys what is necessary and provides ample food, as well as whatever else is necessary to human life. Daily they share the same way of life, the same table, and even the same tastes, all of them loving frugality and hating luxury as a plague for body and soul. And not only do they have a common table, but common clothes also. In fact they have at their disposition thick coats for the winter, and inexpensive tunics for the summer; so it is simple and lawful, for whoever desires to do so, to take the garment he wishes, since it is agreed that whatever belongs to each belongs to all, and conversely, whatever belongs to all belongs to each. In addition, if any of them falls ill he is treated at the expense of the community, and is surrounded by the care and attention of them all. As for the aged, even if they have no children they are as fathers not only of many children but of very good ones. They usually quit life in extremely happy and splendid old age, honoured by privileges and by the regard of so many sons who care for them spontaneously rather than as a result of natural necessity.[7] On the other hand, shrewdly providing against the sole or principal obstacle threatening to dissolve the bonds of communal life, they banned marriage at the same time as they ordered the practice of perfect continence.[8] Indeed, no Essaean takes a woman because women are selfish, excessively jealous, skilful in ensnaring the morals of a spouse and in seducing him by endless charms. Women set out to flatter, and wear all sorts of masks, like actors on the stage; then, when they have bewitched the eye and captured the ear, when, that is to say, they have deceived the lower senses, they next lead the sovereign mind astray.[9] On the other hand, if children are born, they then declare with audacious arrogance, and swollen with pride and effrontery, what they were formerly content to insinuate hypocritically by means of allusions, and shamelessly employ violence to commit actions all of which are contrary to the good of the common life. The husband, bound by his wife's spells, or anxious for his children from natural necessity, is no more the

---

[8] On marriage, cf. Pliny, *Nat. Hist.* 5. 73; *War* 2. 120–1; *Ant.* 18. 21. Contrast *War* 2. 160–1. Also compare 1QS 1.6, but contrast CD 7: 6–7; 1QSa 1: 4; 1QM 7: 4–5.

[9] Misogyny: cf. *War* 2. 121; contrast *War* 2. 161.

ἄλλους ὁ αὐτός ἐστιν, ἀλλ' ἕτερος γέγονε λεληθώς, ἀντ' ἐλευθέρου δοῦλος.

18 οὕτως γοῦν ὁ βίος ἐστὶν αὐτῶν περιμάχητος, ὥστ' οὐκ ἰδιῶται μόνον, ἀλλὰ καὶ μεγάλοι βασιλεῖς ἀγάμενοι τοὺς ἄνδρας τεθήπασι καὶ τὸ σεμνὸν αὐτῶν ἀποδοχαῖς καὶ τιμαῖς ἔτι μᾶλλον σεμνοποιοῦσι.

same towards the others, but unknown to himself he becomes a different man, a slave instead of a freeman.

The life of the Essaeans is indeed so enviable that not only individuals but even great kings are seized with admiration before such men, and are glad to pay homage to their honourable character by heaping favours and honours upon them. 18

2. Pliny the Elder, *Natural History* 5. 17, 4 (73)

Gaius Plinius Secundus, A.D. 23/4–79, was a Roman gentleman from the north Italian town of Comum. A prodigious polymath and a man of practical military and administrative experience, he included a great variety of subjects in his large and diffuse *Natural History*. The *N.H.* was compiled from over 100 principal authors, sometimes carelessly or indiscriminately employed. The extract below comes from the geographical portion of the *N.H.*, where Judaea is described after Egypt along with other areas of Syria. Within a short account of the nature of the Dead Sea—a

73   Ab occidente litora Esseni fugiunt usque qua nocent, gens sola et in toto orbe praeter ceteras mira, sine ulla femina, omni venere abdicata, sine pecunia, socia palmarum. in diem ex aequo convenarum turba renascitur, large frequentantibus quos vita fessos ad mores eorum fortuna fluctibus agit. ita per saeculorum milia—incredibile dictu—gens aeterna est, in qua nemo nascitur. tam fecunda illis aliorum vitae paenitentia est! infra hos Engada oppidum fuit, secundum ab Hierosolymis fertilitate palmetorumque nemoribus, nunc alterum bustum. inde Masada castellum in rupe, et ipsum haut procul Asphaltite. et hactenus Iudaea est.

---

[1] See Dio Chrysostom for the only other independent link of the Essenes with the Dead Sea.
[2] Does Pliny think of the Essenes as a separate nation?

feature of many ancient descriptions of Judaea—can be found the notice of the Essenes. Pliny made a number of errors in the location of places in Judaea and there is no reason to suppose that he knew the region. He does not state his source for his description, but it has been suggested that he may have used for some of it material composed in the reign of Herod or even earlier. At any rate, the depiction in the paragraph below of both Jerusalem and Engedi as burnt suggests that this passage was composed after A.D. 70.

To the west[1] [of the Dead Sea] the Essenes have put the necessary distance between themselves and the insalubrious shore. They are a people[2] unique of its kind and admirable beyond all others in the whole world, without women[3] and renouncing love entirely, without money,[4] and having for company only the palm trees. Owing to the throng of newcomers, this people is daily re-born in equal number; indeed, those whom, wearied by the fluctuations of fortune, life leads to adopt their customs, stream in in great numbers. Thus, unbelievable though this may seem, for thousands of centuries a race has existed which is eternal yet into which no one is born: so fruitful for them is the repentance which others feel for their past lives! Below[5] the Essenes was the town of Engada [Engedi], which yielded only to Jerusalem in fertility and palm-groves but is today become another ash-heap. From there, one comes to the fortress of Masada, situated on a rock, and itself near the lake of Asphalt.

73

---

[3] See *Apol.* 14; *War* 2. 120. Contrast *War* 2. 160–1.
[4] *Q.o.p.* 76; *Apol.* 4; *War* 2. 122.
[5] On the meaning of *infra*, see the Introduction, note 19.

3. Flavius Josephus

Flavius Josephus, c. A.D. 38–after A.D. 93, was a Jewish priest from Jerusalem who participated in and wrote about the great revolt against Rome of A.D. 66–70. A member of the Judaean ruling class, he was appointed by the rebels in the opening years of the war as commander of Jewish forces in Galilee but, captured by the Roman enemy, he aided their cause to such effect that he won his freedom, Roman citizenship and comfortable retirement in Rome. It was there that he undertook the composition of the works which now survive. He is the only Greek or Latin writer to claim personal acquaintance with the Essenes (*Vita* 10), and he certainly had opportunity to learn about all aspects of Jewish culture in Palestine. However, Josephus' desire to present a sympathetic picture of Jews to a gentile audience may have militated against an accurate account and encouraged undue or misleading emphasis on those aspects of Jewish civilization more easily assimilated to the culture of Greek pagans.

(a) Josephus, *The Jewish War*

Published in Greek between A.D. 75 and A.D. 81, this account of the preliminaries, course and consequences of the revolt against

78 Θαυμάσαι δ' ἄν τις ἐν τούτῳ καὶ Ἰούδαν, Ἐσσαῖος ἦν γένος οὐκ ἔστιν ὅτε πταίσας ἢ ψευσθεὶς ἐν τοῖς προαπαγγέλμασιν, ὃς ἐπειδὴ καὶ τότε τὸν Ἀντίγονον ἐθεάσατο παριόντα διὰ τοῦ ἱεροῦ, πρὸς τοὺς γνωρίμους ἀνέκραγεν, ἦσαν δ' οὐκ ὀλίγοι παρεδρεύοντες
79 αὐτῷ τῶν μανθανόντων, »παπαί, νῦν ἐμοὶ καλόν, ἔφη, τὸ θανεῖν, ὅτε μου προτέθνηκεν ἡ ἀλήθεια καί τι τῶν ὑπ' ἐμοῦ προρρηθέντων διέψευσται· ζῇ γὰρ Ἀντίγονος οὑτοσὶ σήμερον ὀφείλων ἀνῃρῆσθαι. χωρίον δὲ αὐτῷ πρὸς σφαγὴν Στράτωνος πύργος εἵμαρτο· καὶ τοῦτο μὲν ἀπὸ ἑξακοσίων ἐντεῦθεν σταδίων ἐστίν, ὧραι δὲ τῆς
80 ἡμέρας ἤδη τέσσαρες· ὁ δὴ χρόνος ἐκκρούει τὸ μάντευμα«. ταῦτα εἰπὼν σκυθρωπὸς ἐπὶ συννοίας ὁ γέρων διεκαρτέρει, καὶ μετ' ὀλίγον ἀνῃρημένος Ἀντίγονος ἠγγέλλετο κατὰ τὸ ὑπόγαιον χωρίον, ὃ δὴ καὶ αὐτὸ Στράτωνος ἐκαλεῖτο πύργος ὁμωνυμοῦν τῇ παραλίῳ Καισαρείᾳ. τοῦτο γοῦν τὸν μάντιν διετάραξεν.

---

[1] See *War* 2. 159 and refs. there.

Rome in A.D. 66–70 tried to blame the outbreak of the war on incompetent Roman governors and a minority of Jewish fanatics. The narrative of Judaean history begins with the Maccabees and is paralleled down to A.D. 66 by Josephus' later work, the *Antiquities*. Josephus published an earlier version of *B.J.* in Aramaic partly for Jews, and it is possible that he expected Jews to read the Greek translation which survives, but his main audience was intended to be Greek and Roman pagans.

(i) *War* 1. 78–80

The event described here was one of the violent episodes of the short rule of the Hasmonaean king Aristobulus I (105–104 B.C.). Aristobulus inherited power from his father John Hyrcanus and, misled by the intrigues of courtiers, was induced to secure his position by ordering his bodyguard to murder his younger brother Antigonus in a dark alleyway in Jerusalem called Strato's Tower. For Josephus' emphasis on Essene proficiency in prophecy, it may be relevant that Josephus himself claimed to be expert at foreseeing the future (*War* 3. 352). See also the parallel account in *Ant.* 13.311.

A remarkable incident in this matter involved Judas. This man was an Essene who had never misled or lied in his prophecies.[1] When Judas saw Antigonus at that time coming through the Temple, he called out to his friends, of whom a fair number of disciples[2] were seated with him: 'Alas, now it is time for me to die since the truth has died on me and one of my foretellings has proved a lie, for Antigonus here is alive although he ought to have been killed today. The place for his decease was fixed by fate as the Tower of Strato, and that tower is a good six hundred stades from here, while the day has reached the fourth hour. The time has rendered invalid the prophecy.' With these words the old man pondered hard with gloomy countenance, and a little later it was announced that Antigonus had been killed in the underground spot which is also called the Tower of Strato, having the same name as Caesarea by the coast. This is what had confused the seer. 78 79 80

[2] The parallel at *Ant.* 13. 311 adds that these disciples were with Simon 'for the purpose of receiving instruction in foretelling the future'.

(ii) *War* 2. 113

This passage is found in the very brief account of the reign of the ethnarch Archelaus. One of the sons of Herod, Archelaus inherited rule over Judaea in 4 B.C. but was dismissed to Gaul by Augustus in A.D. 6. Before his downfall Archelaus had a dream of nine (in *Ant.* 17. 345: ten) tall ears of corn on which oxen were feeding. Simon's interpretation of this dream, described here,

113 ἄλλων δ' ἄλλως ἐξηγουμένων Σίμων τις Ἐσσαῖος τὸ γένος ἔφη τοὺς μὲν στάχυς ἐνιαυτοὺς νομίζειν, βόας δὲ μεταβολὴν πραγμάτων διὰ τὸ τὴν χώραν ἀροτριῶντας ἀλλάσσειν· ὥστε βασιλεύσειν μὲν αὐτὸν τὸν τῶν ἀσταχύων ἀριθμόν, ἐν ποικίλαις δὲ πραγμάτων μεταβολαῖς γενόμενον τελευτήσειν. ταῦτα ἀκούσας Ἀρχέλαος μετὰ πέντε ἡμέρας ἐπὶ τὴν δίκην ἐκλήθη.

[1] For Essenes as a race, see *A.J.* 13. 172; Pliny, *Nat. Hist.* 5. 73.

(iii) *War* 2. 119–161

The description of the three Jewish schools of thought, of which the section on the Essenes constitutes the beginning and much the longest part, is inserted by Josephus into the narrative of the events surrounding the transformation in A.D. 6 of the territory of Archelaus in Judaea into a Roman province under an equestrian governor. The immediate occasion for raising the subject was a reference to the so-called 'Fourth Philosophy', which, according to Josephus, originated in this year in the teachings of the Galilean Judas, who incited the Jews to revolt against Rome. A shorter description of the three philosophies is found in the same context in *Ant.* 18. 11–22, where, however, the description of the Essenes includes important details which are

119 Τρία γὰρ παρὰ Ἰουδαίοις εἴδη φιλοσοφεῖται, καὶ τοῦ μὲν αἱρετισταὶ Φαρισαῖοι, τοῦ δὲ Σαδδουκαῖοι, τρίτον δέ, ὃ δὴ καὶ δοκεῖ σεμνότητα ἀσκεῖν, Ἐσσηνοὶ καλοῦνται, Ἰουδαῖοι μὲν γένος
120 ὄντες, φιλάλληλοι δὲ καὶ τῶν ἄλλων πλέον. οὗτοι τὰς μὲν ἡδονὰς

proved correct. Josephus seems to have lacked good information on the period of Archelaus' rule, and it is probable that the work of Nicolaus of Damascus, used by Josephus for his account of Herod, did not continue this far. The story here is clearly influenced by that of Pharaoh's dream as described in Genesis. For Josephus' own claims to interpret dreams, see *War* 3. 352. See also the parallel to this passage in *Ant*. 17. 345-8.

Many different interpretations were offered but a certain Simon, Essene by race,[1] said that the ears of corn meant years, while the oxen meant a change in affairs as signified by the turning over of the ground which the ploughing produces.[2] Thus he would rule for the number of the years that there were ears of corn but would die enmeshed in a state of confused turmoil. Five days after hearing this Archelaus was called to his trial.

[2] In the parallel account, *Ant*. 17. 347, Josephus adds that the oxen signified pain because the animal is subject to painful labour.

---

missing here but are found also in Philo (the number 4000, rejection of animal sacrifice, Essene interest in agriculture, rejection of slavery). In favour of the hypothesis that the account here was taken from an earlier set piece which may or may not also have been by Josephus is the survival of a similar account in the writings of Hippolytus, since Hippolytus' version includes some small but significant differences from the version in *War*. It is however not impossible that Hippolytus simply altered the *War* account (see below, in the introduction to Hippolytus). The notes point out the main discrepancies between the two descriptions but do not mark the numerous details included by Josephus but not by Hippolytus.

Indeed, there exist among the Jews three schools of philosophy: the Pharisees belong to the first, the Sadducees to the second, and to the third belong men who have a reputation for cultivating a particularly saintly life, called Essenes. They are Jews by race, but in addition they are more closely united among themselves by mutual affection than are

113

119

ὡς κακίαν ἀποστρέφονται, τὴν δὲ ἐγκράτειαν καὶ τὸ μὴ τοῖς πάθεσιν ὑποπίπτειν ἀρετὴν ὑπολαμβάνουσιν. καὶ γάμου μὲν παρ' αὐτοῖς ὑπεροψία, τοὺς δ' ἀλλοτρίους παῖδας ἐκλαμβάνοντες ἁπαλοὺς ἔτι πρὸς τὰ μαθήματα, συγγενεῖς ἡγοῦνται καὶ τοῖς
121 ἤθεσιν αὐτῶν ἐντυποῦσι, τὸν μὲν γάμον καὶ τὴν ἐξ αὐτοῦ διαδοχὴν οὐκ ἀναιροῦντες, τὰς δὲ τῶν γυναικῶν ἀσελγείας φυλαττόμενοι καὶ μηδεμίαν τηρεῖν πεπεισμένοι τὴν πρὸς ἕνα πίστιν.
122 Καταφρονηταὶ δὲ πλούτου, καὶ θαυμάσιον αὐτοῖς τὸ κοινωνικόν, οὐδὲ ἔστιν εὑρεῖν κτήσει τινὰ παρ' αὐτοῖς ὑπερέχοντα· νόμος γὰρ τοὺς εἰς τὴν αἵρεσιν εἰσιόντας δημεύειν τῷ τάγματι τὴν οὐσίαν, ὥστε ἐν ἅπασιν μήτε πενίας ταπεινότητα φαίνεσθαι μήθ' ὑπεροχὴν πλούτου, τῶν δ' ἑκάστου κτημάτων ἀναμεμιγμένων μίαν ὥσπερ
123 ἀδελφοῖς ἅπασιν οὐσίαν εἶναι. κηλῖδα δ' ὑπολαμβάνουσι τὸ ἔλαιον, κἂν ἀλειφθῇ τις ἄκων, σμήχεται τὸ σῶμα· τὸ γὰρ αὐχμεῖν ἐν καλῷ τίθενται λευχειμονεῖν τε διαπαντός. χειροτονητοὶ δ' οἱ τῶν κοινῶν ἐπιμεληταὶ καὶ ἀδιαίρετοι πρὸς ἁπάντων εἰς τὰς χρείας ἕκαστοι.
124 Μία δ' οὐκ ἔστιν αὐτῶν πόλις, ἀλλ' ἐν ἑκάστῃ μετοικοῦσιν πολλοί. καὶ τοῖς ἑτέρωθεν ἥκουσιν αἱρετισταῖς πάντ' ἀναπέπταται τὰ παρ' αὐτοῖς ὁμοίως ὥσπερ ἴδια, καὶ πρὸς οὓς οὐ πρότερον εἶδον
125 εἰσίασιν ὡς συνηθεστάτους· διὸ καὶ ποιοῦνται τὰς ἀποδημίας οὐδὲν μὲν ὅλως ἐπικομιζόμενοι, διὰ δὲ τοὺς λῃστὰς ἔνοπλοι. κηδεμὼν δ' ἐν ἑκάστῃ πόλει τοῦ τάγματος ἐξαιρέτως τῶν ξένων ἀποδείκνυται
126 ταμιεύων ἐσθῆτα καὶ τὰ ἐπιτήδεια. καταστολὴ δὲ καὶ σχῆμα σώματος ὅμοιον τοῖς μετὰ φόβου παιδαγωγουμένοις παισίν. οὔτε δὲ ἐσθῆτας οὔτε ὑποδήματα ἀμείβουσι πρὶν διαρραγῆναι τὸ
127 πρότερον παντάπασιν ἢ δαπανηθῆναι τῷ χρόνῳ. οὐδὲν δ' ἐν ἀλλήλοις οὔτ' ἀγοράζουσιν οὔτε πωλοῦσιν, ἀλλὰ τῷ χρῄζοντι διδοὺς ἕκαστος τὰ παρ' αὐτῷ τὸ παρ' ἐκείνου χρήσιμον ἀντικομίζεται· καὶ χωρὶς δὲ τῆς ἀντιδόσεως ἀκώλυτος ἡ μετάληψις αὐτοῖς παρ' ὧν ἂν θέλωσιν.

---

[1] Adopting children, contrast *Apol*. 3, but cf. 1QSa 1: 4 ff.; CD 15: 5–6.
[2] On Essenes and marriage, see *Apol*. 14–17, and refs. there.
[3] Communism: *Q.o.p.* 85–7; 1QS 1: 11–13; 6: 17, 19 f., 24 f.; 1QpHab 12: 9 f.

the others. The Essenes renounce pleasure as an evil, and regard 120
continence and resistance to the passions as a virtue. They disdain
marriage for themselves, but adopt the children of others at a tender age
in order to instruct them;[1] they regard them as belonging to them by
kinship, and condition them to conform to their own customs. It is not 121
that they abolish marriage, or the propagation of the species resulting
from it, but they are on their guard against the licentiousness of women
and are convinced that none of them is faithful to one man.[2]

They despise riches and their communal life is admirable. In vain 122
would one search among them for one man with a greater fortune than
another. Indeed, it is a law that those who enter the sect shall surrender
their property to the order; so neither the humiliation of poverty nor the
pride of wealth is to be seen anywhere among them. Since their
possessions are mingled, there exists for them all, as for brothers, one
single property.[3] They regard oil as a defilement, and should any of 123
them be involuntarily anointed, he wipes his body clean. They make a
point of having their skin dry and of being always clothed in white
garments.[4] The administrators of the common funds are elected, and
each, without distinction, is appointed in the name of all to the various
offices.[5]

They are not in one town only, but in every town several of them 124
form a colony.[6] Also, everything they have is at the disposal of members
of the sect arriving from elsewhere as though it were their own, and they
enter into the house of people whom they have never seen before as
though they were intimate friends. For this reason also, they carry 125
nothing with them when they travel: they are, however, armed against
brigands.[7] In every town a quaestor of the order, specially responsible
for guests, is appointed steward of clothing and other necessaries. Their 126
dress and outward behaviour are like those of children whose teacher
rears them in fear: they do not change their garments or shoes until they
are completely torn or worn out. They neither buy nor sell anything 127
among themselves; each man gives what he has to whoever needs it, and
receives in return whatever he himself requires. And they can even
receive freely from whomsoever they like without giving anything in
exchange.

---

[4] Contrast the *constant* wearing of white clothes to *V.C.* 66.
[5] Administrators: see *War* 2. 134 and refs. there.
[6] See *Apol.* 1; contrast *Q.o.p.* 76.
[7] Contrast *Q.o.p.* 78, but cf. *V.C.* 24.

128 Πρός γε μὴν τὸ θεῖον εὐσεβεῖς ἰδίως· πρὶν γὰρ ἀνασχεῖν τὸν ἥλιον οὐδὲν φθέγγονται τῶν βεβήλων, πατρίους δέ τινας εἰς αὐτὸν
129 εὐχὰς ὥσπερ ἱκετεύοντες ἀνατεῖλαι. καὶ μετὰ ταῦτα πρὸς ἃς ἕκαστοι τέχνας ἴσασιν ὑπὸ τῶν ἐπιμελητῶν διαφίενται, καὶ μέχρι πέμπτης ὥρας ἐργασάμενοι συντόνως πάλιν εἰς ἓν συναθροίζονται χωρίον, ζωσάμενοί τε σκεπάσμασιν λινοῖς οὕτως ἀπολούονται τὸ σῶμα ψυχροῖς ὕδασιν, καὶ μετὰ ταύτην τὴν ἁγνείαν εἰς ἴδιον οἴκημα συνίασιν, ἔνθα μηδενὶ τῶν ἑτεροδόξων ἐπιτέτραπται παρελθεῖν· αὐτοί τε καθαροὶ καθάπερ εἰς ἅγιόν τι τέμενος
130 παραγίνονται τὸ δειπνητήριον. καὶ καθισάντων μεθ' ἡσυχίας ὁ μὲν σιτοποιὸς ἐν τάξει παρατίθησι τοὺς ἄρτους, ὁ δὲ μάγειρος ἓν
131 ἀγγεῖον ἐξ ἑνὸς ἐδέσματος ἑκάστῳ παρατίθησιν. προκατεύχεται δ' ὁ ἱερεὺς τῆς τροφῆς, καὶ γεύσασθαί τινα πρὶν τῆς εὐχῆς ἀθέμιτον· ἀριστοποιησάμενος δ' ἐπεύχεται πάλιν· ἀρχόμενοί τε καὶ παυόμενοι γεραίρουσι θεὸν ὡς χορηγὸν τῆς ζωῆς. ἔπειθ' ὡς ἱερὰς καταθέμενοι τὰς ἐσθῆτας πάλιν ἐπ' ἔργα μέχρι δείλης τρέπονται.
132 δειπνοῦσι δ' ὁμοίως ὑποστρέψαντες συγκαθεζομένων τῶν ξένων, εἰ τύχοιεν αὐτοῖς παρόντες. οὔτε δὲ κραυγή ποτε τὸν οἶκον οὔτε θόρυβος μιαίνει, τὰς δὲ λαλιὰς ἐν τάξει παραχωροῦσιν ἀλλήλοις.
133 καὶ τοῖς ἔξωθεν ὡς μυστήριόν τι φρικτὸν ἡ τῶν ἔνδον σιωπὴ καταφαίνεται, τούτου δ' αἴτιον ἡ διηνεκὴς νῆψις καὶ τὸ μετρεῖσθαι παρ' αὐτοῖς τροφὴν καὶ ποτὸν μέχρι κόρου.
134 Τῶν μὲν οὖν ἄλλων οὐκ ἔστιν ὅ τι μὴ τῶν ἐπιμελητῶν προσταξάντων ἐνεργοῦσι, δύο δὲ ταῦτα παρ' αὐτοῖς αὐτεξούσια, ἐπικουρία καὶ ἔλεος· βοηθεῖν τε γὰρ τοῖς ἀξίοις, ὁπόταν δέωνται, καὶ καθ' ἑαυτοὺς ἐφίεται καὶ τροφὰς ἀπορουμένοις ὀρέγειν. τὰς δὲ εἰς τοὺς συγγενεῖς μεταδόσεις οὐκ ἔξεστι ποιεῖσθαι δίχα τῶν
135 ἐπιτρόπων. ὀργῆς ταμίαι δίκαιοι, θυμοῦ καθεκτικοί, πίστεως προστάται, εἰρήνης ὑπουργοί. καὶ πᾶν μὲν τὸ ῥηθὲν ὑπ' αὐτῶν ἰσχυρότερον ὅρκου, τὸ δὲ ὀμνύειν αὐτοῖς περιίσταται χεῖρον τῆς ἐπιορκίας ὑπολαμβάνοντες· ἤδη γὰρ κατεγνῶσθαί φασιν τὸν
136 ἀπιστούμενον δίχα θεοῦ. σπουδάζουσι δ' ἐκτόπως περὶ τὰ τῶν

[8] Cf. *V.C.* 27, 89 and below, sect. 148; contrast *Ref.* 9. 21.
[9] Cold water: cf. *War* 2. 138; 1QS 3: 8 f.; 5: 13; 6: 16 f., 22, 25; 7: 3, 16; CD 11: 21 f.
[10] *Apol.* 5; *Q.o.p.* 85.
[11] Are the meals the *thysiai* of *Ant.* 18. 19?
[12] Holy clothes, cf. 1QM 7. 10 f.

The Sources

Their piety towards the Deity takes a particular form: before sunrise they speak no profane word but recite certain ancestral prayers to the sun as though entreating it to rise.[8] After these prayers the superiors dismiss them so that each man may attend to the craft with which he is familiar. Then, after working without interruption until the fifth hour, they reassemble in the same place and, girded with linen loin-cloths, bathe themselves thus in cold water.[9] After this purification they assemble in a special building[10] to which no one is admitted who is not of the same faith; they themselves only enter the refectory if they are pure, as though into a holy precinct. When they are quietly seated, the baker serves out the loaves of bread in order, and the cook serves only one bowlful of one dish to each man. Before the meal the priest says a prayer and no one is permitted to taste the food before the prayer; and after they have eaten the meal he recites another prayer. At the beginning and at the end they bless God as the Giver of life.[11] Afterwards they lay aside the garments which they have worn for the meal, since they are sacred garments,[12] and apply themselves again to work until the evening. Then they return and take their dinner in the same manner, and if guests are passing through they sit at the table. No shouting or disturbance ever defiles the house; they allow each other to speak in turn. To those outside, this silence of the men inside seems a great mystery; but the cause of it is their invariable sobriety and the fact that their food and drink are so measured out that they are satisfied and no more.[13]

On the whole, therefore, they do nothing unless ordered by the superiors.[14] Yet two things depend on themselves: aid and pity. In fact they are allowed on their own discretion to help those worthy of help whenever it is asked for, and to offer food to the needy, but they have no right to subsidize members of their own family without the authority of the procurators. They are righteous arbiters of their anger,[15] masters of their wrath, paragons of loyalty and peacemakers. Every word they speak is stronger than an oath and they refrain from swearing, considering it worse than perjury; for, they say, the man who cannot be believed unless he calls on God as witness condemns himself.[16] They

---

[13] Was this drink wine? Cf. 1QS 6: 4–5; 1QSa 2: 17–22.

[14] See *War* 2. 123, 129; *Ant.* 18. 22; *Apol.* 10. On the Qumran *mebaqer* or *paqid*, see 1QS 6: 12, 19; CD 9: 19, 22; 13: 5–7, 13, 15–16; 14: 10–12; 16: 11.

[15] Self-control: 1QS 5: 25 f.; 6: 25., CD 9: 1–8.

[16] Oath: *Q.o.p.* 84; *Ant.* 15. 371. Contrast *War* 2. 139; cf. CD 9: 1–8; 15: 7–8; 19: 1 f.

42   The Essenes

παλαιῶν συντάγματα μάλιστα τὰ πρὸς ὠφέλειαν ψυχῆς καὶ σώματος ἐκλέγοντες· ἔνθεν αὐτοῖς(πρὸς θεραπείαν παθῶν)ῥίζαι τε ἀλεξητήριον καὶ λίθων ἰδιότητες ἀνερευνῶνται.

137 Τοῖς δὲ ζηλοῦσιν τὴν αἵρεσιν αὐτῶν οὐκ εὐθὺς ἡ πάροδος, ἀλλ' ἐπὶ ἐνιαυτὸν ἔξω μένοντι τὴν αὐτὴν ὑποτίθενται δίαιταν ἀξινάριόν τε καὶ τὸ προειρημένον περίζωμα καὶ λευκὴν ἐσθῆτα δόντες.

138 ἐπειδὰν δὲ τούτῳ τῷ χρόνῳ πεῖραν ἐγκρατείας δῷ, πρόσεισιν μὲν ἔγγιον τῇ διαίτῃ καὶ καθαρωτέρων τῶν πρὸς ἁγνείαν ὑδάτων μεταλαμβάνει, παραλαμβάνεται δὲ εἰς τὰς συμβιώσεις οὐδέπω. μετὰ γὰρ τὴν τῆς καρτερίας ἐπίδειξιν δυσὶν ἄλλοις ἔτεσιν τὸ ἦθος δοκιμάζεται καὶ φανεὶς ἄξιος οὕτως εἰς τὸν ὅμιλον ἐγκρίνεται.

139 πρὶν δὲ τῆς κοινῆς ἅψασθαι τροφῆς ὅρκους αὐτοῖς ὄμνυσι φρικώδεις, πρῶτον μὲν εὐσεβήσειν τὸ θεῖον, ἔπειτα τὰ πρὸς ἀνθρώπους δίκαια φυλάξειν καὶ μήτε κατὰ γνώμην βλάψειν τινὰ μήτε ἐξ ἐπιτάγματος, μισήσειν δ' ἀεὶ τοὺς ἀδίκους καὶ συναγωνιεῖσθαι

140 τοῖς δικαίοις· τὸ πιστὸν ἀεὶ πᾶσιν παρέξειν, μάλιστα δὲ τοῖς κρατοῦσιν· οὐ γὰρ δίχα θεοῦ περιγενέσθαι τινὶ τὸ ἄρχειν· κἂν αὐτὸς ἄρχῃ, μηδέποτε ἐξυβρίσειν εἰς τὴν ἐξουσίαν μηδ' ἐσθῆτί τινι

141 ἢ πλείονι κόσμῳ τοὺς ὑποτεταγμένους ὑπερλαμπρύνεσθαι. τὴν ἀλήθειαν ἀγαπᾶν ἀεὶ καὶ τοὺς ψευδομένους προβάλλεσθαι· χεῖρας κλοπῆς καὶ ψυχὴν ἀνοσίου κέρδους καθαρὰν φυλάξειν καὶ μήτε κρύψειν τι τοὺς αἱρετιστὰς μήθ' ἑτέροις αὐτῶν τι μηνύσειν, κἂν

142 μέχρι θανάτου τις βιάζηται. πρὸς τούτοις ὄμνυσιν μηδενὶ μὲν μεταδοῦναι τῶν δογμάτων ἑτέρως ἢ ὡς αὐτὸς μετέλαβεν, ἀφέξεσθαι δὲ λῃστείας καὶ συντηρήσειν ὁμοίως τά τε τῆς αἱρέσεως αὐτῶν βιβλία καὶ τὰ τῶν ἀγγέλων ὀνόματα. τοιούτοις μὲν ὅρκοις τοὺς προσιόντας ἐξασφαλίζονται.

143 Τοὺς δ' ἐπ' ἀξιοχρέοις ἁμαρτήμασιν ἁλόντας ἐκβάλλουσι τοῦ τάγματος. ὁ δ' ἐκκριθεὶς οἰκτίστῳ πολλάκις μόρῳ διαφθείρεται·

---

[17] Sectarian books? Cf. War 2. 142.
[18] On healing, see Introduction, p. oo, on name of Essenes; cf. V.C. 2.
[19] Cf. 1QS 2: 19–23; 5: 2 f., 23 f.; 6. 8 f.; 1QSa 2: 11 f.; CD 14: 3–6.
[20] Hatchet, see 1QM 7: 6 f.; 11QTS 46: 13–16.
[21] Cf. above, sect. 129.
[22] Cf. above, sect. 123.
[23] Baths, cf. above, sect. 129 and refs. there.

apply themselves with extraordinary zeal to the study of the works of the ancients[17] choosing, above all, those which tend to be useful to body and soul. In them they study the healing of diseases, the roots offering protection and the properties of stones.[18]

Those desiring to enter the sect do not obtain immediate admittance.[19] The postulant waits outside for one year; the same way of life is propounded to him and he is given a hatchet,[20] the loin-cloth which I have mentioned,[21] and a white garment.[22] Having proved his continence during this time, he draws closer to the way of life and participates in the purificatory baths[23] at a higher degree, but he is not yet admitted into intimacy. Indeed, after he has shown his constancy, his character is tested for another two years, and if he appears worthy he is received into the company permanently.[24] But before touching the common food he makes solemn vows before his brethren.[25] He first swears to practise piety towards the Deity; then to observe justice towards men and to do no wrong to any man, neither of his own accord nor at another's command; to hate the wicked always,[26] and to fight together with the just.[27] He swears constant loyalty to all, but above all to those in power; for authority never falls to a man without the will of God. He swears never to show insolence in the exercise of his duty should he ever happen to be in command himself, nor to outshine his subordinates in his dress or by increased adornment. He swears always to love truth and to pursue liars; to keep his hands pure from theft and his soul pure from wicked gain. Also he swears to conceal nothing from the members of the sect, and to reveal nothing to outsiders even though violence unto death be used against him.[28] In addition, he swears to transmit none of the doctrines except as he himself received them, to abstain from robbery, and to preserve in like manner both the books of their sect and the names of the Angels. Such are the oaths by which they secure the fidelity of those who enter the sect.

Those who are caught in the act of committing grave faults are expelled from the order.[29] The individual thus excluded often perishes,

137
138
139
140
141
142
143

---

[24] Probation in general: contrast 1QS 5: 7–13; 6: 13–23; 7: 18–21; CD 13: 11–13; 15: 5 f.
[25] On initiatory oath, see 1QS 1: 16–17; 5: 1–11; 6: 14–15; CD 15: 5–6; 1QH 14: 17 f.
[26] Contrast *Ref.* 9. 23.
[27] Compare this list to *Q.o.p.* 83 and refs. there.
[28] Secrecy: cf. 1QS 4: 6; 5: 15 f.; 9: 16 f., 21 f.
[29] Expulsion: cf. 1QS 7: 1 f., 16 f., 22–5; 8: 21–9: 2.

τοῖς γὰρ ὅρκοις καὶ τοῖς ἔθεσιν ἐνδεδεμένος οὐδὲ τῆς παρὰ τοῖς ἄλλοις τροφῆς δύναται μεταλαμβάνειν, ποηφαγῶν δὲ καὶ λιμῷ τὸ
144 σῶμα τηκόμενος διαφθείρεται. διὸ δὴ πολλοὺς ἐλεήσαντες ἐν ταῖς ἐσχάταις ἀναπνοαῖς ἀνέλαβον, ἱκανὴν ἐπὶ τοῖς ἁμαρτήμασιν αὐτῶν τὴν μέχρι θανάτου βάσανον ἡγούμενοι.
145 Περὶ δὲ τὰς κρίσεις ἀκριβέστατοι καὶ δίκαιοι, καὶ δικάζουσι μὲν οὐκ ἐλάττους τῶν ἑκατὸν συνελθόντες, τὸ δ' ὁρισθὲν ὑπ' αὐτῶν ἀκίνητον. σέβας δὲ μέγα παρ' αὐτοῖς μετὰ τὸν θεὸν τοὔνομα τοῦ νομοθέτου, κἂν βλασφημήσῃ τις εἰς τοῦτον κολάζεται θανάτῳ.
146 τοῖς δὲ πρεσβυτέροις ὑπακούουσιν καὶ τοῖς πλείοσιν ἐν καλῷ· δέκα γοῦν συγκαθεζομένων οὐκ ἂν λαλήσειέν τις ἀκόντων τῶν ἐννέα.
147 καὶ τὸ πτύσαι δὲ εἰς μέσους ἢ τὸ δεξιὸν μέρος φυλάσσονται καὶ ταῖς ἑβδομάσιν ἔργων ἐφάπτεσθαι διαφορώτατα Ἰουδαίων ἁπάντων· οὐ μόνον γὰρ τροφὰς ἑαυτοῖς πρὸ μιᾶς ἡμέρας παρασκευάζουσιν, ὡς μὴ πῦρ ἐναύοιεν ἐκείνην τὴν ἡμέραν, ἀλλ' οὐδὲ
148 σκεῦός τι μετακινῆσαι θαρροῦσιν οὐδὲ ἀποπατεῖν. ταῖς δ' ἄλλαις ἡμέραις βόθρον ὀρύσσοντες βάθος ποδιαῖον τῇ σκαλίδι, τοιοῦτον γάρ ἐστιν τὸ διδόμενον ὑπ' αὐτῶν ἀξινίδιον τοῖς νεοσυστάτοις, καὶ περικαλύψαντες θοἰμάτιον, ὡς μὴ τὰς αὐγὰς ὑβρίζοιεν τοῦ θεοῦ,
149 θακεύουσιν εἰς αὐτόν. ἔπειτα τὴν ἀνορυχθεῖσαν γῆν ἐφέλκουσιν εἰς τὸν βόθρον· καὶ τοῦτο ποιοῦσι τοὺς ἐρημοτέρους τόπους ἐκλεγόμενοι. καίπερ δὴ φυσικῆς οὔσης τῆς τῶν λυμάτων ἐκκρίσεως ἀπολούεσθαι μετ' αὐτὴν καθάπερ μεμιασμένοις ἔθιμον.
150 Διῄρηνται δὲ κατὰ χρόνον τῆς ἀσκήσεως εἰς μοίρας τέσσαρας, καὶ τοσοῦτον οἱ μεταγενέστεροι τῶν προγενεστέρων ἐλαττοῦνται, ὥστ' εἰ ψαύσειαν αὐτῶν, ἐκείνους ἀπολούεσθαι καθάπερ ἀλλοφύλῳ
151 συμφυρέντας. καὶ μακρόβιοι μέν, ὡς τοὺς πολλοὺς ὑπὲρ ἑκατὸν παρατείνειν ἔτη, διὰ τὴν ἁπλότητα τῆς διαίτης ἔμοιγε δοκεῖν καὶ τὴν εὐταξίαν, καταφρονηταὶ δὲ τῶν δεινῶν, καὶ τὰς μὲν ἀλγηδόνας νικῶντες τοῖς φρονήμασιν, τὸν δὲ θάνατον, εἰ μετ' εὐκλείας
152 πρόσεισι, νομίζοντες ἀθανασίας ἀμείνονα. διήλεγξεν δὲ αὐτῶν ἐν ἅπασιν τὰς ψυχὰς ὁ πρὸς Ῥωμαίους πόλεμος, ἐν ᾧ στρεβλούμενοί τε καὶ λυγιζόμενοι καιόμενοί τε καὶ κλώμενοι καὶ διὰ πάντων ὁδεύοντες τῶν βασανιστηρίων ὀργάνων, ἵν' ἢ βλασφημήσωσιν τὸν νομοθέτην ἢ φάγωσίν τι τῶν ἀσυνήθων, οὐδέτερον ὑπέμειναν παθεῖν, ἀλλ' οὐδὲ κολακεῦσαί ποτε τοὺς αἰκιζομένους ἢ δακρῦσαι.

[30] Court: cf. 1QS 6: 24 f.; 1QSa 1: 25 f.; CD 14: 3 f.
[31] Cf. 1QS 5: 8; 8: 15, 22; 1QS 1: 3; cf. 9. 9.
[32] Spitting: cf. 1QS 7: 13.

the prey to a most miserable fate; for bound by his oaths and customs he cannot even share the food of others. Reduced to eating grass, he perishes, his body dried up by hunger. They have also out of compassion taken back many who were at their last gasp, judging this torture to death sufficient for the expiation of their faults. 144

In matters of judgement they are very exact and impartial. They dispense justice at assemblies of not less than a hundred, and their decisions are irrevocable.[30] The name of the Lawgiver is, after God, a great object of veneration among them, and if any man blasphemes against the Lawgiver he is punished with death.[31] They make it their duty to obey their elders as well as the majority; for example, when ten men sit together no man speaks if the other nine oppose it. In addition they refrain from spitting in the middle of the company, or to the right.[32] They are also forbidden, more rigorously than any other Jew, to attend to their work on the seventh day. Not only do they prepare their food on the day before to avoid lighting a fire on that day, but they dare not even move an object, or go to stool.[33] On other days, they dig a hole one foot deep with their mattocks (for such is the hatchet given to the new disciples). They squat there, covered by their mantles so as not to offend the rays of God.[34] Then they push back the excavated soil into the hole. For this operation they choose the loneliest places. However natural the evacuation of excrement, they are accustomed to wash themselves afterwards as though defiled. 145 146 147 148 149

They are divided into four lots according to the duration of their discipline, and the juniors are so inferior to their elders that if the latter touch them they wash themselves as though they had been in contact with a stranger.[35] I think it is because of the simplicity of their way of life and their regularity that they live long, so that most of them reach the age of more than a hundred years. Yet they despise danger: they triumph over pain by the heroism of their convictions, and consider death, if it come with glory, to be better than preservation of life. The war against the Romans fully revealed their souls. During it their limbs were twisted and broken, burned and shattered; they were subjected to every instrument of torture to compel them either to blaspheme against the Lawgiver or to eat forbidden food. But they refused to do either, or even to flatter their butchers or weep. Smiling amidst pain, and mocking 150 151 152 153

---

[33] Shabbat: cf. *Q.o.p.* 81; CD 10: 14–11: 18.
[34] The sun? Cf. above, sect. 128.
[35] On the four classes, contrast *Ref.* 9. 26.

153 μειδιῶντες δὲ ἐν ταῖς ἀλγηδόσιν καὶ κατειρωνευόμενοι τῶν τὰς βασάνους προσφερόντων εὔθυμοι τὰς ψυχὰς ἠφίεσαν ὡς πάλιν κομιούμενοι.
154 Καὶ γὰρ ἔρρωται παρ' αὐτοῖς ἥδε ἡ δόξα, φθαρτὰ μὲν εἶναι τὰ σώματα καὶ τὴν ὕλην οὐ μόνιμον αὐτῶν, τὰς δὲ ψυχὰς ἀθανάτους ἀεὶ διαμένειν, καὶ συμπλέκεσθαι μὲν ἐκ τοῦ λεπτοτάτου φοιτώσας αἰθέρος ὥσπερ εἱρκταῖς τοῖς σώμασιν ἴυγγί τινι φυσικῇ κατασπω-
155 μένας, ἐπειδὰν δὲ ἀνεθῶσι τῶν κατὰ σάρκα δεσμῶν, οἷα δὴ μακρᾶς δουλείας ἀπηλλαγμένας τότε χαίρειν καὶ μετεώρους φέρεσθαι. καὶ ταῖς μὲν ἀγαθαῖς ὁμοδοξοῦντες παισὶν Ἑλλήνων ἀποφαίνονται τὴν ὑπὲρ ὠκεανὸν δίαιταν ἀποκεῖσθαι καὶ χῶρον οὔτε ὄμβροις οὔτε νιφετοῖς οὔτε καύμασι βαρυνόμενον, ἀλλ' ὃν ἐξ ὠκεανοῦ πραῢς ἀεὶ ζέφυρος ἐπιπνέων ἀναψύχει· ταῖς δὲ φαύλαις ζοφώδη καὶ χειμέριον
156 ἀφορίζονται μυχὸν γέμοντα τιμωριῶν ἀδιαλείπτων. δοκοῦσι δέ μοι κατὰ τὴν αὐτὴν ἔννοιαν Ἕλληνες τοῖς τε ἀνδρείοις αὐτῶν, οὓς ἥρωας καὶ ἡμιθέους καλοῦσιν, τὰς μακάρων νήσους ἀνατεθεικέναι, ταῖς δὲ τῶν πονηρῶν ψυχαῖς καθ' ᾅδου τὸν ἀσεβῶν χῶρον, ἔνθα καὶ κολαζομένους τινὰς μυθολογοῦσιν, Σισύφους καὶ Ταντάλους Ἰξίονάς τε καὶ Τιτυούς, πρῶτον μὲν ἀιδίους ὑφιστάμενοι τὰς
157 ψυχάς, ἔπειτα εἰς προτροπὴν ἀρετῆς καὶ κακίας ἀποτροπήν. τούς τε γὰρ ἀγαθοὺς γίνεσθαι κατὰ τὸν βίον ἀμείνους ἐλπίδι τιμῆς καὶ μετὰ τὴν τελευτήν, τῶν τε κακῶν ἐμποδίζεσθαι τὰς ὁρμὰς δέει προσδοκώντων, εἰ καὶ λάθοιεν ἐν τῷ ζῆν, μετὰ τὴν διάλυσιν
158 ἀθάνατον τιμωρίαν ὑφέξειν. ταῦτα μὲν οὖν Ἐσσηνοὶ περὶ ψυχῆς θεολογοῦσιν ἄφυκτον δέλεαρ τοῖς ἅπαξ γευσαμένοις τῆς σοφίας αὐτῶν καθιέντες.
159 Εἰσίν δ' ἐν αὐτοῖς οἳ καὶ τὰ μέλλοντα προγινώσκειν ὑπισχνοῦνται, βίβλοις ἱεραῖς καὶ διαφόροις ἁγνείαις καὶ προφητῶν ἀποφθέγμασιν ἐμπαιδοτριβούμενοι· σπάνιον δ' εἴ ποτε ἐν ταῖς προαγορεύσεσιν ἀστοχοῦσιν.
160 Ἔστιν δὲ καὶ ἕτερον Ἐσσηνῶν τάγμα, δίαιταν μὲν καὶ ἔθη καὶ νόμιμα τοῖς ἄλλοις ὁμοφρονοῦν, διεστὼς δὲ τῇ κατὰ γάμον δόξῃ· μέγιστον γὰρ ἀποκόπτειν οἴονται τοῦ βίου μέρος, τὴν διαδοχήν, τοὺς μὴ γαμοῦντας, μᾶλλον δέ, εἰ πάντες τὸ αὐτὸ φρονήσειαν,

---

[36] On the soul and immortality, contrast *Ref.* 9. 27.
[37] On study of the holy books, cf. *Q.o.p.* 80–2.

those who tortured them, they gave up their souls cheerfully, convinced that they would recover them again.

Indeed, it is a firm belief among them that although bodies are corruptible, and their matter unstable, souls are immortal and endure for ever; that, come from subtlest ether, they are entwined with the bodies which serve them as prisons, drawn down as they are by some physical spell; but that when they are freed from the bonds of the flesh, liberated, so to speak, from long slavery, then they rejoice and rise up to the heavenly world. Agreeing with the sons of the Greeks, they declare that an abode is reserved beyond the Ocean for the souls of the just; a place oppressed neither by rain nor snow nor torrid heat, but always refreshed by the gentle breeze blowing from the Ocean. But they relegate evil souls to a dark pit shaken by storms, full of unending chastisement.[36] The Greeks, I think, had the same idea when they assigned their valiant ones, whom they call 'heroes' and 'demi-gods', to the Islands of the Blessed, and the souls of the bad to Hades, the place of the wicked, where according to their mythology, certain people such as Sisyphus, Tantalus, Ixion and Tityus, undergo their torment. A belief of this kind assumes in the first place that souls are eternal; next, it serves to encourage virtue and to deflect from vice. Indeed, the good will become better during their lives if they hope to be rewarded, even after their end; whilst the wicked will restrain their instincts out of fear if they expect to suffer eternal punishment after their dissolution even though they escape while they live. Such, then, are the religious teachings of the Essenes with regard to the soul: they offer them as a lure, and those who have once tasted their wisdom do not resist.

There are some among them who, trained as they are in the study of the holy books[37] and the different sorts of purifications, and the sayings of the prophets, become expert in foreseeing the future: they are rarely deceived in their predictions.[38]

There exists another order of Essenes who, although in agreement with the others on the way of life, usages, and customs, are separated from them on the subject of marriage. Indeed, they believe that people who do not marry cut off a very important part of life, namely, the propagation of the species; and all the more so that if everyone adopted the same opinion the race[39] would very quickly disappear.[40]

[38] Prophecy: cf. *War* 1. 78–80; 2. 113; *Ant.* 15. 373–8; 1Qp Hab 6: 3–5.
[39] Compare *Ref.* 9. 28: 'the whole of mankind'.
[40] Marriage: contrast *Apol.* 14 and refs. there.

161 ἐκλιπεῖν ἂν τὸ γένος τάχιστα. δοκιμάζοντες μέντοι τριετίᾳ τὰς γαμετάς, ἐπειδὰν τρὶς καθαρθῶσιν εἰς πεῖραν τοῦ δύνασθαι τίκτειν, οὕτως ἄγονται. ταῖς δ' ἐγκύμοσιν οὐχ ὁμιλοῦσιν, ἐνδεικνύμενοι τὸ μὴ δι' ἡδονὴν ἀλλὰ τέκνων χρείαν γαμεῖν. λουτρὰ δὲ ταῖς γυναιξὶν ἀμπεχομέναις ἐνδύματα, καθάπερ τοῖς ἀνδράσιν ἐν περιζώματι. τοιαῦτα μὲν ἔθη τοῦδε τοῦ τάγματος.

(iv) *War* 2. 567; 3. 11
The first passage narrates the appointment of new generals by the Jewish rebels in Jerusalem in October A.D. 66 after the defeat of Roman forces under Cestius Gallus. Under the new government of the independent Jewish state districts were assigned to individual commanders, one of whom was Josephus himself, who

567 Ἠμέλουν δὲ οὐδὲ τῆς ἄλλης χώρας, ἀλλ' εἰς μὲν Ἱεριχοῦν Ἰώσηπος ὁ Σίμωνος, εἰς δὲ τὴν Περαίαν Μανασσῆς, Θαμνᾶ δὲ τοπαρχίας Ἰωάννης ὁ Ἐσσαῖος στρατηγήσων ἐπέμφθη· προσκεκλήρωτο δ' αὐτῷ Λύδδα καὶ Ἰόππη καὶ Ἀμμαοῦς.

* * * * *

11 Ἐξηγοῦντο δὲ τῆς καταδρομῆς τρεῖς ἄνδρες ἀλκήν τε κορυφαῖοι καὶ συνέσει, Νίγερ τε ὁ Περαΐτης καὶ ὁ Βαβυλώνιος Σίλας, πρὸς οἷς Ἰωάννης ὁ Ἐσσαῖος.

(v) *War* 5. 145
This is part of Josephus' long description of Jerusalem which immediately precedes his narrative of the siege of the city in A.D. 70. The immediate context is the account of the three walls around the city. It is the most ancient wall whose position is plotted in this extract. This is the only place in ancient literature where the gate of the Essenes is mentioned, and its precise

145 Κατὰ θάτερα δὲ πρὸς δύσιν, ἀπὸ ταὐτοῦ μὲν ἀρχόμενον, διὰ δὲ τοῦ Βησοῦ καλουμένου χώρου κατατεῖνον ἐπὶ τὴν Ἐσσηνῶν πύλην, κἄπειτα πρὸς νότον ὑπὲρ τὴν Σιλωὰν ἐπιστρέφον πηγήν, ἔνθεν δὲ πάλιν ἐκκλῖνον πρὸς ἀνατολὴν ἐπὶ τὴν Σολομῶνος κολυμβήθραν καὶ διῆκον μέχρι χώρου τινός, ὃν καλοῦσιν Ὀφλάς, τῇ πρὸς ἀνατολὴν στοᾷ τοῦ ἱεροῦ συνῆπτε.

The Sources

Nevertheless, they observe their women for three years. When they have 161
purified themselves three times and thus proved themselves capable of
bearing children, they then marry them. And when they are pregnant
they have no intercourse with them, thereby showing that they do not
marry for pleasure but because it is necessary to have children. The
women bathe wrapped in linen, whereas the men wear a loin-cloth.
Such are the customs of this order.

---

took over Galilee. A certain John the Essene was given authority
in the north and west of Judaea. It is perhaps surprising that he is
next mentioned (in the second passage) as one of the leaders of an
attack on Ascalon in the south during which, according to *War* 3.
19, he was killed in battle. For Essene participation in the revolt,
see *War* 2. 152–3.

Nor did they neglect the rest of the country. To Jericho went Joseph 567
son of Simon and to Peraea went Manasses. John the Essene was sent to
be general over the toparchy of Thamna, and Lydda, Joppa and
Ammaus were added to his area.

* * * * *

Three men of exceptional strength and intelligence led the expedition: 11
Niger the Peraean and the Babylonian Silas, along with John the Essene.

---

position has not been identified. On the reason for the name, the
best hypotheses are that the gate lay in a quarter particularly
inhabited by Essenes, or that it was the gate through which they
used to leave the city to relieve themselves if they felt that the
holy city, like the camp (cf. *War* 2. 148), should not be polluted
by their natural functions.

In the other direction going towards the west and starting from the same 145
place, it stretched down through the place called Beso to the gate of
Essenes, then turned back southwards over the Siloan fountain, then
bent back to the east towards the pool of Solomon and led, via a place
which they call Ophlas, until it reached the eastern portico of the
Temple.

(b) Josephus, *Antiquities of the Jews*

The *Antiquities*, completed in c. A.D. 93, was a long work in twenty books composed by Josephus to inform a gentile audience about Jewish history in the hope that a demonstration of the Jews' ancient origins might encourage admiration of, and tolerance for, their customs. The first half of the composition is a paraphrase of the biblical narrative. Fewer sources survived for

(i) *Ant.* 13. 171–2
This brief reference to the Jewish sects comes in the narrative of the foreign relations of the Hasmonaean dynasty in the time of Jonathan (161–143/2 B.C.) during his struggle for independence from the Seleucid kings of Syria. It is inserted immediately after

171   Κατὰ δὲ τὸν χρόνον τοῦτον τρεῖς αἱρέσεις τῶν Ἰουδαίων ἦσαν, αἳ περὶ τῶν ἀνθρωπίνων πραγμάτων διαφόρως ὑπελάμβανον, ὧν ἡ μὲν Φαρισαίων ἐλέγετο, ἡ δὲ Σαδδουκαίων, ἡ τρίτη δὲ Ἐσσηνῶν.
172   οἱ μὲν οὖν Φαρισαῖοι τινὰ καὶ οὐ πάντα τῆς εἱμαρμένης ἔργον εἶναι λέγουσιν, τινὰ δ' ἐφ' ἑαυτοῖς ὑπάρχειν συμβαίνειν τε καὶ μὴ γίνεσθαι. τὸ δὲ τῶν Ἐσσηνῶν γένος πάντων τὴν εἱμαρμένην κυρίαν ἀποφαίνεται καὶ μηδὲν ὃ μὴ κατ' ἐκείνης ψῆφον ἀνθρώποις ἀπαντᾶν.

[1] Cf. Pliny, *Nat. Hist.* 5. 73.

(ii) *Ant.* 15. 371–9
This passage occurs in Josephus' description of the methods used by Herod at the height of his power (from c. 20 B.C.) to control his subjects. This included the requirement that all the

371   Ἀφείθησαν δὲ ταύτης τῆς ἀνάγκης καὶ οἱ παρ' ἡμῖν Ἐσσαῖοι καλούμενοι· γένος δὲ τοῦτ' ἔστιν διαίτῃ χρώμενον τῇ παρ' Ἕλλησιν ὑπὸ Πυθαγόρου καταδεδειγμένῃ. περὶ τούτων μὲν οὖν ἐν
372   ἄλλοις σαφέστερον διέξειμι. τοὺς δὲ Ἐσσηνοὺς ἀφ' οἵας αἰτίας

[1] On Essene reluctance to take oaths, cf. *War* 2. 135 and refs. there.

his use for the period after 440 B.C., and for some of his account he was compelled to rely on popular Jewish traditions and stories written by non-Jews rather than on any Jewish text. There is a marked increase in his knowledge where information was available to him from the writings of Nicolaus of Damascus, the court historian of Herod the Great.

---

the description of an embassy sent to Sparta to make an alliance and before the narrative of an attack on Jonathan by the generals of the Seleucid monarch Demetrius II. It appears quite incongruous in this context and it is obscure why Josephus inserted it here.

At this time there were three sects of the Jews which took different attitudes to human affairs. One sect was called the Pharisees, another the Sadducees and the third was the Essenes. The Pharisees say that some things but not everything are the work of fate, while some things either happen or do not because of the actions of individuals. The race[1] of the Essenes, by contrast, makes Fate mistress of all and says that nothing comes to pass for humans unless Fate has so voted.[2]

171
172

[2] On fate (or providence), cf. *Ant.* 18. 18; 1QS 3: 13–4: 26.

---

population should take an oath of loyalty. The disciples of Pollion the Pharisee and Samaias refused on principle but were not punished out of Herod's regard for Pollion. Josephus explains here why the Essenes also were excused.

Among those spared from being forced to do this[1] were also those we call Essenes, a group which employs the same daily regime as was revealed to the Greeks by Pythagoras.[2] I shall give a clearer account of these people in other places. But it is worth saying here what caused him

371
372

[2] Cf. *Ref.* 9. 27. See also *Life* 12 for Pharisees compared to Stoics.

ἐτίμα μεῖζόν τι φρονῶν ἐπ' αὐτοῖς ἢ κατὰ τὴν θνητὴν φύσιν, εἰπεῖν ἄξιον· οὐ γὰρ ἀπρεπὴς ὁ λόγος φανεῖται τῷ τῆς ἱστορίας γένει παραδηλῶν καὶ τὴν ὑπὲρ τούτων ὑπόληψιν. Ἦν τις τῶν Ἐσσηνῶν Μανάημος ὄνομα καὶ τἆλλα κατὰ τὴν προαίρεσιν τοῦ βίου καλοκαγαθίαν μαρτυρούμενος καὶ πρόγνωσιν ἐκ θεοῦ τῶν μελλόντων ἔχων. οὗτος ἔτι παῖδα τὸν Ἡρώδην εἰς διδασκάλου φοιτῶντα κατιδὼν βασιλέα Ἰουδαίων προσηγόρευσεν. ὁ δ' ἀγνοεῖν ἢ κατειρωνεύεσθαι νομίζων αὐτὸν ἀνεμίμνησκεν ἰδιώτης ὤν. Μανάημος δὲ μειδιάσας ἠρέμα καὶ τύπτων τῇ χειρὶ κατὰ τῶν γλουτῶν »ἀλλά τοι καὶ βασιλεύσεις, ἔφη, καὶ τὴν ἀρχὴν εὐδαιμόνως ἀπάξεις· ἠξίωσαι γὰρ ἐκ θεοῦ. καὶ μέμνησο τῶν Μαναήμου πληγῶν, ὥστε σοι καὶ τοῦτο σύμβολον εἶναι τῶν κατὰ τὴν τύχην μεταπτώσεων. ἄριστος γὰρ ὁ τοιοῦτος λογισμός, εἰ καὶ δικαιοσύνην ἀγαπήσειας καὶ πρὸς τὸν θεὸν εὐσέβειαν ἐπιείκειαν δὲ πρὸς τοὺς πολίτας· ἀλλ' οὐ γὰρ οἶδά σε τοιοῦτον ἔσεσθαι τὸ πᾶν ἐπιστάμενος. εὐτυχίᾳ μὲν γὰρ ὅσον οὐκ ἄλλος διοίσεις καὶ τεύξῃ δόξης αἰωνίου, λήθην δ' εὐσεβείας ἕξεις καὶ τοῦ δικαίου. ταῦτα δ' οὐκ ἂν λάθοι τὸν θεὸν ἐπὶ τῇ καταστροφῇ τοῦ βίου τῆς ἀντ' αὐτῶν ὀργῆς ἀπομνημονευομένης.« τούτοις αὐτίκα μὲν ἥκιστα τὸν νοῦν προσεῖχεν ἐλπίδι λειπόμενος αὐτῶν Ἡρώδης, κατὰ μικρὸν δὲ ἀρθεὶς ἕως καὶ τοῦ βασιλεύειν καὶ εὐτυχεῖν ἐν τῷ μεγέθει τῆς ἀρχῆς μεταπέμπεται τὸν Μανάημον καὶ περὶ τοῦ χρόνου πόσον ἄρξει διεπυνθάνετο. Μανάημος δὲ τὸ μὲν σύμπαν οὐκ εἶπεν· ὡς δὲ σιωπῶντος αὐτοῦ, μόνον εἰ δέκα γενήσονται βασιλείας ἐνιαυτοὶ προσεπύθετο καὶ εἴκοσι καὶ τριάκοντα εἰπὼν τὸν ὅρον οὐκ ἐπέθηκε τῷ τέλει τῆς προθεσμίας, Ἡρώδης δὲ καὶ τούτοις ἀρκεσθεὶς τόν τε Μανάημον ἀφῆκεν δεξιωσάμενος καὶ πάντας ἀπ' ἐκείνου τοὺς Ἐσσηνοὺς τιμῶν διετέλει. ταῦτα μὲν οὖν εἰ καὶ παράδοξα δηλῶσαι τοῖς ἐντυγχάνουσιν ἠξιώσαμεν καὶ περὶ τῶν παρ' ἡμῖν ἐμφῆναι, διότι πολλοὶ {διὰ} τοιούτων ὑπὸ καλοκαγαθίας καὶ τῆς τῶν θείων ἐμπειρίας ἀξιοῦνται.

---

[3] On prophecy, cf. *War* 2. 159 and refs. there.
[4] The text here is emended slightly.

[Herod] to honour the Essenes and have an opinion of them greater than was to be expected given their mortal nature. Such an explanation is not unfitting in the genre of history and it will also clarify these men's reputation.

There was a certain Essene whose name was Manaemus. He bore witness to his virtue in the whole conduct of his life and especially in his possession from God of knowledge of the future.[3] This man once saw Herod when the latter, still a boy, was on the way to his teacher's house, and addressed him as 'king of the Jews'. Herod thought he was either ignorant or joking and reminded him that he was a private citizen. But Manaemus smiled gently and tapped him with his hand on the rump, saying: 'But indeed you will be king and you will rule[4] happily, for you have been found worthy by God. And remember how Manaemus struck you so that this may be a symbol to you of the changes brought by fortune. For it would be most sensible if you were to love justice, piety to God and decency to the citizens, but I know that you will not be like that for I know everything. You will be picked out for greater good fortune than any other man and you will achieve eternal fame, but you will forget piety and justice. But this cannot escape the notice of God, and at the conclusion of your life his anger for these things will be called to his mind.' At the time Herod paid little heed to these words since he had no hope of such things, but when he had been raised little by little to the kingship and good fortune, at the peak of his power he sent for Manaemus and asked him what would be the length of his rule. Manaemus remained totally silent. In the face of such silence Herod asked him simply whether ten would be the years of his rule. He replied that they would be twenty or thirty but that he put no limit to the end of the appointed time. Herod, satisfied with this, treated him honourably and sent him away, and from that time always treated all Essenes with respect. These things may seem unbelievable but we have thought it right to report them to the reader and to make known what goes on among us, for many are thought worthy of such things because of their goodness and knowledge of divine matters.[5]

373
374
375
376
377
378
379

---

[5] Text uncertain. The Loeb edition translates: 'Many of these men have indeed been vouchsafed a knowledge of divine things because of their virtue'.

(iii) *Ant.* 18. 18-22
This passage is inserted within Josephus' account of the Roman transformation of Judaea into a province in A.D. 6. The three main Jewish philosophies are described in order to contrast them with the new Fourth Philosophy which instigated unrest against Rome in that year. The passage is therefore parallel to *War* 2.

18 Ἐσσηνοῖς δὲ ἐπὶ μὲν θεῷ καταλείπειν φιλεῖ τὰ πάντα ὁ λόγος, ἀθανατίζουσιν δὲ τὰς ψυχὰς περιμάχητον ἡγούμενοι τοῦ δικαίου
19 τὴν πρόσοδον. εἰς δὲ τὸ ἱερὸν ἀναθήματα στέλλοντες θυσίας ἐπιτελοῦσιν διαφορότητι ἁγνειῶν, ἃς νομίζοιεν, καὶ δι' αὐτὸ εἰργόμενοι τοῦ κοινοῦ τεμενίσματος ἐφ' αὑτῶν τὰς θυσίας ἐπιτελοῦσιν. βέλτιστοι δὲ ἄλλως {ἄνδρες} τὸν τρόπον καὶ τὸ πᾶν
20 πονεῖν ἐπὶ γεωργίᾳ τετραμμένοι. ἄξιον δ' αὐτῶν θαυμάσαι παρὰ πάντας τοὺς ἀρετῆς μεταποιουμένους τόδε διὰ τὸ μηδαμῶς ὑπάρξαν Ἑλλήνων ἢ βαρβάρων τισίν, ἀλλὰ μηδ' εἰς ὀλίγον, ἐκείνοις ἐκ παλαιοῦ συνελθὸν ἐν τῷ ἐπιτηδεύεσθαι μὴ κεκωλῦσθαι· τὰ χρήματά τε κοινά ἐστιν αὐτοῖς, ἀπολαύει δὲ οὐδὲν ὁ πλούσιος τῶν οἰκείων μειζόνως ἢ ὁ μηδ' ὁτιοῦν κεκτημένος· καὶ τάδε
21 πράσσουσιν ἄνδρες ὑπὲρ τετρακισχίλιοι τὸν ἀριθμὸν ὄντες. καὶ οὔτε γαμετὰς εἰσάγονται οὔτε δούλων ἐπιτηδεύουσιν κτῆσιν, τὸ μὲν εἰς ἀδικίαν φέρειν ὑπειληφότες, τὸ δὲ στάσεως ἐνδιδόναι ποίησιν, αὐτοὶ δ' ἐφ' ἑαυτῶν ζῶντες διακονίᾳ τῇ ἐπ' ἀλλήλοις
22 ἐπιχρῶνται. ἀποδέκτας δὲ τῶν προσόδων χειροτονοῦντες καὶ ὁπόσα ἡ γῆ φέροι ἄνδρας ἀγαθούς, ἱερεῖς δὲ ἐπὶ ποιήσει σίτου τε καὶ βρωμάτων. ζῶσι δὲ οὐδὲν παρηλλαγμένως, ἀλλ' ὅτι μάλιστα ἐμφέροντες Δακῶν τοῖς πλείστοις λεγομένοις.

[1] Cf. *Ant.* 13. 172. On fate, see 1QS 3: 13-14: 26.
[2] The epitome of Josephus and the Latin version place a negative before ἐπιτελοῦσιν, with the meaning: 'offer no sacrifices since the purifications to which they are accustomed are different'. On sacrifices, compare and contrast *Q.o.p.* 75; 1QS 9: 3-5; CD 6: 11-20; 11: 17-21; 16: 13 f.
[3] Are these the sacred meals described at *War* 2. 129-32?
[4] Cf. *Apol.* 8; *Q.o.p.* 78, where it is stated what crafts are not practised.
[5] The Greek text is difficult to understand.
[6] For the number, cf. *Q.o.p.* 75.
[7] On slaves, cf. *Q.o.p.* 79 and refs. there.

The Sources

119–166, to which Josephus explicitly refers the reader at *Ant.* 18. 11. The account here is both much shorter and different in content to that in *War*. Most of the details peculiar to this passage are also found in Philo, *Q.o.p.*, on which Josephus may have drawn.

The Essenes like to teach that in all things one should rely on God.[1] They also declare that souls are immortal, and consider it necessary to struggle to obtain the reward of righteousness. They send offerings to the Temple, but perform their sacrifices using different customary purifications.[2] For this reason, they are barred from entering into the common enclosure, but offer sacrifice among themselves.[3] For the rest, they are excellent men and wholly given up to agricultural labour.[4] Compared to all others adept in virtue, their practice of righteousness is admirable; nothing similar ever existed in any Greek or any barbarian even for a short time, yet among them it has prevailed unimpeded from a remote age.[5] They put their property into a common stock, and the rich man enjoys no more of his fortune than does the man with absolutely nothing. And there are more than 4000 men who behave in this way.[6] In addition, they take no wives and acquire no slaves;[7] in fact, they consider slavery an injustice, and marriage as leading to discord.[8] They therefore live among themselves and serve each other. They choose virtuous men to collect the revenue[9] and gather the various products of the soil, and priests to prepare the bread and food.[10] They live in no way different from, but as much as possible like, the so-called majority of the Dacians.[11]

18

19

20

21

22

---

[8] On marriage, cf. *Apol.* 14–17 and refs. there.

[9] See *War* 2. 123 and refs. at *War* 2. 134. Cf. also 1QS 1: 9 f.; 6: 4f; 1QSa 2: 11–22 etc.

[10] The Greek *could* mean that the bakers and cooks are selected from members of an hereditary priesthood or that the Essenes elected their priests. Cf. *War* 2. 130–1.

[11] The Greek text here does not make good sense. Ortelius emended πλείστοις to Κτίσταις (a Dacian tribe). Dupont-Sommer proposed Σαδδουκαίων in place of Δακῶν. Neither suggestion is very satisfactory.

(c) Josephus, *Life* 10–11

The autobiography of Josephus was composed to answer accusations by his enemies that he had participated too wholeheartedly in the war against Rome in A.D. 66–7. It was added to the *Antiquities* when the latter work was published in c. A.D. 93. This passage is found in the brief account of the author's origins and upbringing which is placed at the beginning of the book.

10 Περὶ δὲ ἐκκαίδεκα ἔτη γενόμενος ἐβουλήθην τῶν παρ' ἡμῖν αἱρέσεων ἐμπειρίαν λαβεῖν· τρεῖς δὲ εἰσὶν αὗται, Φαρισαίων μὲν ἡ πρώτη, καὶ Σαδδουκαίων ἡ δευτέρα, τρίτη δ' Ἐσσηνῶν, καθὼς πολλάκις εἴπομεν· οὕτως γὰρ ᾤμην αἱρήσεσθαι τὴν ἀρίστην, εἰ
11 πάσας καταμάθοιμι. σκληραγωγήσας οὖν ἐμαυτὸν καὶ πολλὰ πονηθεὶς τὰς τρεῖς διῆλθον.

It is immediately followed by a description of Josephus' further instruction at the hands of an ascetic called Bannus, with whom Josephus claims that he spent three years (*Life* 12) before deciding to adhere to the Pharisaic persuasion. It is hard to see how so long a period can be fitted into the chronology of Josephus' life, and it may be suspected that his description of his education has been idealised.

At about the age of sixteen I wished to get experience of the schools of thought to be found among us. There are three of these—Pharisees the first, Sadducees the second, Essenes the third—as we have often remarked. I thought that in this way, by learning about all of them, I would choose the best. I therefore made myself hardy and, with much trouble, went through the three courses.

4. Dio of Prusa, in Synesius of Cyrene, *Dio* 3, 2

Dio Cocceianus, later called Chrysostomos, *c.* A.D. 40 to after 112, was a renowned Greek orator and popular Stoic-Cynic philosopher from Bithynia in modern Turkey. Many of his discourses survive but the present extract comes from the biography of Dio composed *c.* A.D. 400 by Synesius of Cyrene (*c.* A.D. 370–413), a Neoplatonist orator who became a bishop near the end of his life. It is likely that Dio mentioned the Essenes

Ἔτι καὶ τοὺς Ἐσσηνοὺς ἐπαινεῖ που, πόλιν ὅλην εὐδαίμονα τὴν παρὰ τὸ νεκρὸν ὕδωρ ἐν τῇ μεσογείᾳ τῆς Παλαιστίνης κειμένην παρ' αὐτά που τὰ Σόδομα.

[1] Allocation of a city to the Essenes is not found elsewhere.

only in passing, in one of his lost speeches. They could have fitted in well with his promulgation of stock Stoic concepts of virtue and philanthropy. Dio travelled widely but there is no good reason to believe that he visited Palestine; if he did so, it is unlikely that the Qumran community still existed. Dio's account is similar to Pliny's, but it is not close enough to suggest either that he derived his information from Pliny or that they had a common source.

Also somewhere he praises the Essenes, who form an entire and prosperous city[1] near the Dead Sea, in the centre of Palestine, not far from Sodom.[2]

---

[2] Opinion on the precise location of Sodom differed in ancient sources. Strabo, Geog. 16. 2. 44, placed it at the south end of the Dead Sea; Philo, *De Abrahamo* 14, put it at the north.

5. Hegesippus, *Hypomnemata*, in Eusebius, *Ecclesiastical History* IV 22. 7

A Christian author of ecclesiastical history in the second century A.D., Hegesippus was a converted Jew and probably a native of Palestine. His *Hypomnemata* ('Memoirs') were written in two books to combat Gnostic heretics within the Church and he does not seem to have had any particular interest in discussing Jews.

Ἔτι δ' ὁ αὐτὸς καὶ τὰς πάλαι γεγενημένας παρὰ' Ἰουδαίοις αἱρέσεις ἱστορεῖ λέγων· ἦσαν δὲ γνῶμαι διάφοροι ἐν τῇ περιτομῇ ἐν υἱοῖς Ἰσραηλιτῶν κατὰ τῆς φυλῆς Ἰούδα καὶ τοῦ Χριστοῦ αὗται· Ἐσσαῖοι Γαλιλαῖοι Ἡμεροβαπτισταὶ Μασβωθεοι Σαμαρεῖται Σαδδουκαῖοι Φαρισαῖοι.

His work now survives only in fragments, of which nearly all those extant are preserved in Eusebius' *Ecclesiastical History*. It was characteristic of Eusebius (*c*. A.D. 260–340) to quote authorities and documents in his history and it can be assumed that Hegesippus' text is accurately reproduced, despite its apparently confused nature.

The same author further discusses the sects which in earlier times existed among the Jews, as follows: 'There were differing opinions in the circumcision among the children of Israel about the tribe of Judah and the Christ, as follows: Essaeans, Galileans, Hemerobaptists, Masbotheans, Samaritans, Sadducees, Pharisees.'

6. Hippolytus of Rome, *Refutation of all Heresies* 9. 18-28

Hippolytus, *c.* A.D. 170–*c.* 236, was a Roman presbyter and (probably) rival bishop to Callistus of Rome from A.D. 217 to 222. The *Refutation of all Heresies* was his chief work, planned to show how the Christian heresies described in Books 5–10 were the offspring of the Greek philosophical systems described in the earlier books. Books 4–10 were found in a manuscript of Mt Athos in the nineteenth century and ascribed to Origen under the title *Philosophumena*, but it is now generally accepted as the work of Hippolytus. By the time of Hippolytus the notion that deviant ideas should be excluded from the body of the Church as heresy was well advanced, but this notion had only gradually evolved during the first century and a half after the crucifixion. The Essenes were viewed anachronistically by Hippolytus and other Christian writers as breakaway, deviant Jews, although the earlier sources do not portray them as at odds with the Jewish mainstream. There is no certainty either about Hippolytus' source or about the value of his account. It is very close to the description of the Essenes by Josephus, *War* 2. 119–161, and it is

18 Τρία γὰρ παρ' αὐτοῖς εἴδη διαιρεῖται, καὶ τοῦ μὲν αἱρετισταί εἰσι Φαρισαῖοι, τοῦ δὲ Σαδδουκαῖοι, τρίτοι δὲ Ἐσ⟨σ⟩ηνοί. οὗτοι τὸν βίον σεμνότερον ἀσκοῦσι, φιλάλληλοι ὄντες καὶ ἐγκρατεῖς, πάσης τε ἐπιθυμίας ἔργον ἀποστρέφονται, ἀπεχθῶς καὶ πρὸς ⟨τὸ⟩ τὰ τοιαῦτα ἀκ(ο)ῦσαι ἔχοντες, γάμον τε ἀπαγορεύουσι. τοὺς δὲ ἀλλοτρίους παῖδας ἀναλαμβάνοντες τεκνοποιοῦνται καὶ πρὸς τὰ ἴδια ἤθη ἄγουσιν, οὕτως ἀνατρέφοντες καὶ ἔτι τοῖς μαθήμασι προβιβάζοντες, οὐ τὸ γαμεῖν κωλύοντες, ἀλλ' αὐτοὶ γάμου ἀπεχόμενοι. γυναῖκας δέ, εἰ καὶ τῇ αὐτῇ προαιρέσει βούλοιντο προσέχειν, οὐ προσδέχονται, κατὰ μηδένα τρόπον γυναιξὶ πιστεύοντες.

19 Καταφρονοῦσι δὲ πλούτου καὶ τὸ πρὸς τοὺς δεομένους κοινωνεῖν οὐκ ἀποστρέφο(ντ)αι, ἀλλ' οὐδέ τις παρ' αὐτοῖς ὑπὲρ τὸν ἕτερον πλουτεῖ. ν(ό)μος γὰρ παρ' αὐτοῖς / τὸν προσιόντα τῇ αἱρέσει τὰ

The Sources

not impossible that it derived directly from that text, but in that case it is hard to account for all the divergences from Josephus' version. Not all the discrepancies can easily be explained by any Christianizing intentions of the author, for Hippolytus did not usually alter the material he excerpted except by omission or condensation and he was in general concerned to discredit the sects he described, not to Christianize them. One alternative suggestion would be that Hippolytus and Josephus drew upon a common source composed either by a Jew or an informed gentile before A.D. 70, in which case Hippolytus' independent testimony to that source would be of the utmost importance. On the other hand, the divergences could also be explained by the hypothesis that Hippolytus may have used a paraphrase of Josephus' passage written by a Christian author of the second century A.D. Notes for those passages where Hippolytus and Josephus give more or less the same account may be found at the relevant places in *War*; since the descriptions follow the same order, it has not been thought necessary to supply cross-references here to the parallel material in *War*, but only to point out the main differences.

18   For there is a division amongst them into three types, and the adherents of the first sect are the Pharisees, but of the second the Sadducees, while the third are Essenes. These practise a more devotional life, being filled with mutual love and being temperate. They turn away from every act of inordinate desire, being averse even to hearing things of the sort,[1] and they renounce matrimony. They take the boys of others and have offspring begotten for them whom they lead into an observance of their own peculiar customs, and in this way bring them up and impel them to learn their teachings. They do not forbid marriage but they themselves refrain from matrimony. Women, however, even though they may be disposed to adhere to the same course of life, they do not admit, for in no way whatsoever have they confidence in women.

19   They despise wealth and do not turn away from sharing with those that are destitute, but not even one amongst them enjoys a greater amount of riches than another. For a regulation with them is that an

---

[1] Detail not found in *War* 2. 120.

ὑπάρχοντα πωλοῦντα ⟨τὰ χρήματα⟩ τῷ κοινῷ προσφέρειν· ἃ
ὑποδεχόμενος ⟨ὁ⟩ ἄρχων διανέμει ἅπασι πρὸς τὰ δέοντα· οὕτως
οὐδ(εἰ)ς ἐνδεὴς παρ' αὐτοῖς. ἐλαίῳ δὲ οὐ χρῶνται, μολυσμὸν
ἡγούμ(ενοι) τὸ ἀλ(εί)φεσθαι. χειροτονοῦνται δὲ οἱ ἐπιμεληταί, οἱ
πάντων ⟨τῶν⟩ κοινῶ(ν) (φ)ρο(ντί)ζ(ο)ντ(ες). πάντες δὲ ἀεὶ
λευχειμονοῦσι.
20 Μία δὲ αὐτῶν οὐκ ἔστι πόλι(ς), ἀλλ' ἐν ἑκάστῃ μετοικοῦσι
πολλοί. καὶ εἴ τις ἀπὸ ξένης παρῇ τῶν αἱρετιστῶν, πάντα αὐτῷ
κοινὰ ἡγοῦνται, καὶ οὓς οὐ πρότερον ᾔδεσαν, ὡς οἰκείους καὶ
συνήθεις προσδέχονται. περιῖασι δὲ τὴν πατρῴαν γῆν ἑκάστοτε
ἀποδημοῦντες μηδὲν φέροντες πλὴν ὅπλου. ἔχουσι δὲ καὶ κατὰ
πόλεις προεστῶτα, ὃς τὰ συναγόμενα εἰς τοῦτο ἀναλίσκει, ἐσθῆτα
καὶ τροφὰς αὐτοῖς παρασκευάζων. καταστολὴ δὲ αὐτῶν καὶ σχῆμα
κόσμιον. χιτῶνας δὲ δύο ἢ διπλᾶς ὑποδέσεις οὐ κτῶνται· ἐπὰν δὲ
τὰ παρόντα παλαιωθῇ, τότε ἕτερα προσίενται. οὐδὲν δὲ ὅλως οὔτε
ἀγοράζουσιν οὔτε πωλοῦσιν, ὃ δ' ἂν ἔχῃ τις τῷ μὴ ἔχοντι δούς, ὃ
οὐκ ἔχει λαμβάνει.
21 Παραμένουσι δὲ εὐτάκτως καὶ ἐπιμόνως εὐχόμενοι ἔωθεν,
μηδὲν πρότερον φθεγξ(ά)μενοι εἰ μὴ τὸν θεὸν ὑμνήσωσι· καὶ
οὕτω, προ⟨σ⟩ελθόντες ἕκ(α)στοι ἐφ' ὃ βούλονται, πράττουσι, καὶ
ἕως ὥρας πέμπτης πράξαντες ἐπανίασιν. ἔπειτα πάλιν συνελθόντες
εἰς ἕνα τόπον, περιζώμασί τε λινοῖς περιζωσάμενοι—πρὸς τὸ
καλύψασθαι τὴν αἰσχύνην—, οὕτως ὕδατι ψυχρῷ ἀπολούονται. καὶ
μετὰ τὸ οὕτως ἁγνίσασθαι εἰς ἓν οἴκημα συνίασιν—οὐδεὶς δὲ
⟨τῶν⟩ ἑτέρ(ο)δόξων σύνεισιν ἐν τῷ οἴκῳ—καὶ περὶ ἀριστοποιΐαν
χωροῦσι. καθισάντων δὲ κατὰ τάξιν μεθ' ἡσυχίας / προσφέρονται
ἄρτοι, ἔπειτα ἕν τι προσφάγιον, ἐξ οὗ ἑκάστῳ τὸ αὔταρκες μέρος.
οὐ πρότερον δὲ γεύ(σετ)αί (τις) (α)ὐτῶν, εἰ μὴ ἐπ(εύ)ξεται
εὐλογῶν ὁ ἱερεύς. μετὰ (δὲ) τὸ ἄριστον ἐπεύχεται πάλιν· ἀρχόμενοί τε καὶ [πάλιν] παυόμενοι ὑμνοῦσι τὸν θεόν. ἔπειτα τὰς
ἐσθῆτας, (ἅ)ς (ἔν)δ(ον) συνεστιώμενοι ἀμφιέν⟨ν⟩υνται,
ἀποθέμεν(οι) ὡ(ς) (ἱ)εράς—εἰσὶ δὲ λιναῖ—⟨καὶ⟩ τὰς ἐν τῇ
προόδῳ πάλιν ἀναλαμβάνοντες ἐπὶ τὰ φίλα ἔργα ὁρμῶσιν ἕως

---

[2] Contrast *War* 2. 128.
[3] Contrast *War* 2. 129.

individual joining the sect must sell his possessions and present the money to the community; on receiving which, the ruler distributes it to all according to their necessities. Thus there is no one among them in distress. They do not use oil, regarding it as a defilement to be anointed. There are appointed overseers, who take care of all things that belong to them in common, and they all always appear in white clothing.

There is not one city of them, but they settle in every town and are numerous. And if any of the adherents of the sect may be present from a foreign city, they consider that all things are in common for him, and those whom they had not previously known they receive as if they belonged to their own household and kindred. They traverse their native land, and on each occasion that they go on a journey they carry nothing except arms. And they have also in their cities a president, who expends the moneys collected for this purpose in procuring clothing and food for them. Their robe and its shape are modest. They do not own two cloaks or a double set of shoes, but when those that are in present use become antiquated, then they adopt others. They neither buy nor sell anything at all, but whatever any one has he gives to him that has not, and that which he has not he receives.

They continue in an orderly manner and with perseverance pray from early dawn, not speaking a word until they have praised God in a hymn.[2] And in this way they act, each going to whatever employment they please,[3] and after having worked up to the fifth hour they leave off. Then again they come together into one place, girdling themselves with linen girdles to conceal their private parts.[4] In this manner they perform ablutions in cold water, and after being thus cleansed, they repair together into one apartment—no one who entertains a different opinion from themselves being with them in the house—and proceed to partake of breakfast. When they have taken their seats in order and in silence, the loaves are set out, and next some one sort of food to eat along with it, and each receives from these a sufficient portion. No one, however, will taste these before the priest utters a blessing and prayer over them. After breakfast, he again says a prayer: as at the beginning, so at the conclusion of their meal they hymn God. Next, after they have laid aside as sacred the garments in which they have been clothed while together taking their repast within—now these garments are linen—and having resumed the clothes in the vestibule,[5] they hasten to agreeable

---

[4] Explanation not found in *War* 2. 129.
[5] Detail not found in *War* 2. 131.

δείλης. δειπνοῦσι δὲ ὁμοίως τοῖς προειρημένοις πάντα ποιήσαντες. οὐδεὶς δὲ πώποτε κραυγάσει ἤ τις ἑτέρα θορυβώδης ἀκουσθήσεται φωνή, ἠρέμα δὲ ἕκαστοι λαλοῦντες εὐσχημόνως ἕτερος τῷ ἑτέρῳ τὴν ὁμιλίαν συγχωρεῖ, ὡς τοῖς ἔξωθεν μυστήριόν τι καταφαίνεσθαι τὴν τῶν ἔνδον σιωπήν. νήφουσι δὲ πάντοτε, πάντα μέτρῳ καὶ ἐσθίοντες καὶ πίνοντες.

22 Πάντες μὲν οὖν τῷ προεστῶτι προσέχουσι καὶ ὅσ' ἂ⟨ν⟩ κελεύσῃ ὡς νόμῳ πείθονται. ἐσπουδάκασι δὲ πρὸς τὸ ἐλεεῖν καὶ βοηθεῖν τοῖς καταπονουμένοις. πρὸ δὲ πάντων ὀργῆς ἀπέχουσι καὶ θυμοῦ καὶ πάντων τῶν ὁμοίων, ἐπίβουλα ταῦτα τοῦ ἀνθρώπου κρίνοντες. οὐδεὶς δὲ ὄμνυσι παρ' αὐτοῖς, ὅσα δ' ἄν τις εἴπῃ, τοῦτο ὅρκου ἰσχυρότερον κρίνεται· εἰ δὲ ὀμόσει τις, καταγινώσκεται ⟨ἤδη, φασίν,⟩ ὡς μὴ πιστευθεὶς ⟨δίχα θεοῦ⟩. σπουδάζουσι δὲ περὶ τὰς τοῦ νόμου ἀναγνώσεις καὶ προφητῶν, ἔτι δὲ καὶ εἴ τι σύνταγμα εἴη ⟨τῶν⟩ πιστῶν. πάνυ δὲ περιέργως ἔχουσι περὶ βοτάνας καὶ λίθους, περιεργότεροι ὄντες πρὸς τὰς τούτων ἐνεργείας, φάσκοντες μὴ μάτην ταῦτα γεγονέναι.

23 Τοῖς δὲ βουλομένοις τῇ αἱρέσει μαθ(η)τεύ(ειν) οὐκ εὐθέως τὰς παραδόσεις ποιοῦνται, εἰ μὴ πρό(τ)ερον δοκ(ι)μά/σωσιν· ἐπ' ἐνιαυτὸν γὰρ ⟨αὐτοῖς⟩ τὰς ὁμοίας τροφὰς παρατιθέασιν, ἔξω τῆς ἑαυτῶν σ(υνό)δου (οὖ)σιν ἐν ἑτέρῳ οἴκῳ, ἀξινάριόν τε καὶ τὸ λινοῦν περίζωμα κα(ὶ) (λ)ευκὴν ἐσ(θ)ῆτα δόντες. ἐπειδὰν ⟨δὲ⟩ τούτῳ τῷ χρόνῳ πεῖραν (ἐ)γκρα(τεί)ας δῷ, πρόσεισιν ἔγγιον τῇ διαίτῃ καὶ καθαρωτέρως ἀπολ(ούετα)ι ἢ τὸ πρότερον, οὐδέπω δὲ σὺν αὐτοῖς ⟨τῆς⟩ τροφῆς μεταλαμβάνει. μετὰ γὰρ τὸ δεῖξαι εἰ ἐγκρατεύεσθαι δύναται, ἐπὶ ἔτη ἄλλα δύο δοκιμάζεται τοῦ τοιούτου [γὰρ] τὸ ἦθος, καὶ φανεὶς ἄξιος οὕτως εἰς αὐτοὺς ⟨ἐγ⟩κρίνεται.

Πρὶν δὲ αὐτοῖς συνεστιαθῇ, ὅρκοις φρικτοῖς ὁρκίζεται· πρῶτον μὲν εὐσεβήσειν τὸ θεῖον, ἔπειτα τὰ πρὸς ἀνθρώπους δίκαια φυλάξειν καὶ κατὰ μηδένα τρόπον ἀδικήσειν τινά· μηδένα τε μήτε ἀδικοῦντα μήτε ἐχθρὸν μισήσειν, προσεύχεσθαι δὲ ὑπὲρ αὐτῶν, ⟨καὶ⟩ συναγωνίζεσθαι [αὐτῶν] τοῖς δικαίοις. τὸ πιστὸν πᾶσι

---

[6] Explanation not found in *War* 2. 135.
[7] The mss. do not have δίχα θεοῦ, which is inserted here by Marcovich from *War* 2. 135.

occupations until evening. They partake of supper, doing all things in like manner to those already mentioned. No one will at any time cry aloud, nor will any other tumultuous voice be heard, but they each converse quietly, and with decorum one concedes the conversation to the other, so that the stillness of those within appears a sort of mystery to those outside. They are invariably sober, both eating and drinking all things by measure.

All then pay attention to the president, and whatever injunctions he may issue, they obey as law. For they are anxious that mercy and assistance be extended to those who are burdened with toil. Especially they abstain from wrath and anger, and all such passions, considering these to be treacherous to man.[6] No one amongst them is in the habit of swearing, but whatever any one says, this is regarded more binding than an oath. If, however, one will swear, he is indeed condemned, they say, on the grounds that without God[7] he was not believed. They are solicitous about the readings of the law and prophets and, furthermore, over any treatise of the faithful. They evince the utmost curiosity concerning plants and stones, rather busying themselves as regards the operative powers of these, saying that these things were not created in vain.[8] 22

But to those who wish to become disciples of the sect, they do not immediately deliver their rules, unless they have previously tested them. For the space of a year they set before them the same sorts of food, while they continue to live in a different house outside the Essenes' own place of meeting. They give to them a hatchet and the linen girdle and a white robe. When, at the expiration of this period, one affords proof of self-control, he approaches nearer to their method of living and is washed more purely than before. Not as yet, however, does he partake of the food along with them. For, after having furnished evidence as to whether he is able to acquire self-control—but for two years the character of such a person is tested—and when he has appeared deserving, then is he reckoned amongst the members. 23

But before he is allowed to partake of a repast along with them, he is bound under fearful oaths. First, that he will worship the Divinity; next, that he will observe just dealings with men, and that he will in no way injure any one; next, that he will not hate a person who injures him, or is hostile to him, but pray for them,[9] and that he will aid the just. He

---

[8] Explanation not found in *War* 2. 136.
[9] Contrast *War* 2. 139.

⟨μὲν⟩ παρέξειν, μάλιστα ⟨δὲ⟩ τοῖς κρατοῦσιν· οὐ γὰρ δίχα θεοῦ συμβαίνει⟨ν⟩ τινὶ τὸ ἄρχειν. κἂν αὐτὸς ἄρχῃ, μηδέποτε ὑπερηφανεύσασθαι ἐν ⟨τῇ⟩ ἐξουσίᾳ, μηδὲ ἀγ⟨λαοῖς⟩ ἐσθήσε⟨σ⟩ιν ἢ τινι κόσμῳ πλείον⟨ι⟩ τοῦ ⟨συν⟩ήθους χρήσασθαι. φιλαλήθη τε ⟨ἀεὶ⟩ εἶναι, τὸν δὲ ψευδόμ(εν)ο(ν) ἐλέγχειν· μηδὲ κλέπτειν μηδὲ συνείδησιν ἐπὶ ἀνόμῳ κέρδει μολύνειν. ⟨καὶ⟩ μηδὲν ἀποκρύπτειν τοὺς συναιρεσιώτας, ἑτέροις δὲ μηδὲν ἐξειπεῖν, κἂν μέχρι θανάτου τις βιάζηται. πρὸς τούτοις ὄμνυσι μη(δ)ενὶ μεταδοῦναι τῶν δογμάτων ἑτέρως ἢ ὡς αὐτὸς μετέλαβε.

24 Τοιούτοις οὖν ὅρκοις δεσ(μεύο)υσι τ(οὺς) προσερχομένους. εἰ δέ τις ἐν ἁμαρτήματί τιν(ι) (μεγάλῳ ληφθ)ῇ, ἀποβάλλεται τοῦ δώματος, ὁ δὲ ἀ/ποβληθεὶς δεινῷ μόρῳ ἔσθ' ὅτε διαφθείρεται. τοῖς γὰρ ὅρκοις καὶ τοῖς ἔθεσιν ἐνδεδεμένος, (οὐ)δὲ τῆς παρὰ τοῖς ἄλλοις τροφῆς δύναται μεταλ(α)μβάνειν. ἔσθ' ὅτε οὖν τὸ σῶμα λιμῷ δι(α)φθείρ(ο)υσιν· (ὅθ)εν ἐν ἐσχάτοις ποτὲ ⟨ὄντας καὶ⟩ (ἤδ)η ἐκλείποντας ἐλεοῦσι πολλούς, ⟨τῶν ἁμαρτημάτων⟩ αὐτῶν ἱκανὴν ⟨τὴν⟩ μέχρι θανάτου ἐπιτιμίαν ἡγούμενοι.

25 Περὶ δὲ τὰς κρίσεις ἀκριβέστατοι καὶ δίκαιοι· δικάζουσι δὲ συνελθόντες οὐκ ἐλάττους τῶν ἑκατόν, τὸ δὲ ὁρισθὲν ὑπ' αὐτῶν ἀκίνητον. τιμῶσι δὲ τὸν νομοθέτην μετὰ τὸν θεὸν ⟨μάλιστα⟩, καὶ εἴ τις εἰς τοῦτον βλασφημήσει, κολάζεται ⟨θανάτῳ⟩. τοῖς δὲ ἄρχουσι καὶ πρεσβυτέροις ὑπακούειν διδάσκονται. εἰ δὲ ἐπὶ τὸ αὐτὸ δέκα καθέζονται, οὐ λαλήσει εἷς, εἰ μὴ τοῖς ἐννέα δόξει. καὶ τὸ πτύσαι δὲ εἰς μέσον ἢ τὸ δεξιὸν μέρος φυλάττονται. τὸ δὲ τῷ σαββάτῳ ἀπέχεσθαι ἔργου φροντίζουσι μᾶλλον πάντων Ἰουδαίων· οὐ μόνον γὰρ τροφὰς αὑτοῖς παρασκευάζονται ⟨πρὸ⟩ μιᾶς ἡμέρας—πρὸς τὸ μὴ πῦρ ἅπτειν—, ἀλλ' οὐδὲ σκεῦός ⟨τι⟩ μετατιθέασιν οὐδὲ ἀποπατήσουσι—τινὲς δὲ οὐδὲ κλινιδίου χωρίζονται. —ταῖς δὲ ἄλλαις ἡμέραις ἐπὰν ἀποπατῆσαι θέλοιεν, βόθρον ὀρύξαντες ποδιαῖον τῇ σκαλίδι—τοιοῦτον γάρ ἐστι τὸ ἀξινάριον, ὃ

---

[10] The mss. do not have θανάτῳ, which is inserted here by Marcovich from *War* 2. 145.

swears to keep faith with all, but especially with those who are rulers, on the grounds that a position of authority does not happen to any one without the will of God. And he swears that if he himself be a ruler, he will not conduct himself at any time arrogantly in power, nor resort to fine clothes or any adornment greater than the norm. He swears always to be a lover of truth, and to reprove him that is guilty of falsehood, neither to steal, nor pollute his conscience for the sake of iniquitous gain, and he swears not to conceal anything from those who are members of his sect, and to divulge nothing to others, though he should be tortured even to death. In addition to the foregoing, he swears to impart to no one a knowledge of the doctrines in a different manner from that in which he has received them himself.

With oaths, then, of this description, they bind those who come to them. If, however, any one may be caught in any great sin, he is expelled from the house, and one that has been thus expelled sometimes perishes by an awful death. For, since he is bound by the oaths and rites, he is not able to partake of the food in use among other people. Occasionally, therefore, they suffer total physical destruction through starvation. And so it is, that when they are sometimes in extremities and at the point of dissolution, in many cases the Essenes have pity on them, since they deem a punishment unto death a sufficient penalty for their transgressions.

But as regards judicial decisions, they are most accurate and impartial. They deliver their judgements after assembling to the number of at least one hundred, and the sentence delivered by them is irreversible. They particularly honour the legislator after God, and if any one is guilty of blasphemy against this individual, he is punished with death.[10] They are taught to yield obedience to rulers and elders. If ten sit down in the same place, no one will speak until it appears expedient to the other nine, and they are careful not to spit out into the middle or to the right. They are more solicitous about abstaining from work on the Sabbath day than all Jews. For not only do they prepare their food for themselves one day previously, so as not to kindle a fire, but they would not even move a utensil from one place to another, nor ease themselves; some would not even rise from a couch.[11] On other days, however, when they wish to relieve nature, they dig a hole a foot long with the mattock (for of this description is the hatchet, which they

---

[11] Detail not found in *War* 2. 147.

τοις προσιουσι μαθητεύεσθαι πρώτως διδόασι—και περικαλύψαντες το ιμάτιον ιζάνουσι, φάσκοντες μη δειν υβρίζειν τας
αυγάς ⟨του θεου⟩· έπειτα την ανασκαφεισαν γην
επεμβάλ⟨λ⟩ουσιν εις τ(ο)ν βόθρον· και τουτο ποιουσιν
εκλεγ(όμεν)οι (τους) ερημοτέρους τόπους. επάν δε τουτ(ο)
(ποιήσωσ)ιν, / ευθύς απολούονται, ως μιαινούσης της εκκρίσεως.

26 Διήρηνται δε (κ)ατά (χρ)όνον και ουχ ομοίως την άσκησιν
φυλάττουσιν, εις τέσσ(αρ)α μέρη διαχωρισθέντες. —έτεροι γαρ
αυτών τα υπέρ το δέον (α)σκουσιν, ως μηδέ νόμισμα βαστάζειν,
λέγοντ(ες) μη δειν ει(κό)να η φέρειν η οράν η ποιειν· διο ουδέ εις
πόλιν τι(ς) αυτών εισπορεύεται, ίνα μη δια πύλης εισέλθη, εφ' η
ανδριάντες έπεισιν, αθέμιτον τουτο ηγούμενος το υπό εικόνας
παρελθειν. έτεροι δέ, επάν ακούσωσί τινος περί θεου διαλεγομένου
και των τούτου νόμων, ει απερίτμητος είη, παραφυλάξας ⟨τις
αυτών⟩ τον τοιουτον εν τόπω τινί μόνον, φονεύειν απειλει ει μη
περιτμηθείη· ου, ει μη βούλοιτο πείθεσθαι, ου φείδεται αλλά και
σφάζει· όθεν εκ του συμβαίνοντος ⟨και⟩ το όνομα προσέλαβον,
Ζηλωταί καλούμενοι, υπό τινων δε Σικάριοι. έτεροι δε αυτών
ουδένα κύριον ονομάζουσι πλην τον θεόν, ει και αικίζοιτό τις
⟨αυτών⟩ η και αναιροιτο. —τοσου(το)ν δε οι μετέπειτα ελάττους
τη ασκήσει γεγένη⟨ν⟩ται, ώστε τους τοις αρχαίοις έθεσιν εμμέν-
οντας μηδέ προσψαύειν αυτών· ων ει ψαύσαιεν, ευθέως απολούονται, ώς τινος αλλοφ(ύ)λ(ου) ψαύσαντες.

Εισί δε και μακρόβιοι οι πλείστοι, ώστε και πλέον ⟨η⟩ εκατόν
έτεσι ζην· φα(σιν) ουν ⟨τούτου⟩ είναι αίτιον τό τε της άκρας
θεοσεβείας ⟨αυτών⟩ και το (κ)αταγνωσθη⟨ναι⟩ ⟨του⟩ αμέτρως
προσφέρεσθαι ⟨τη διαίτη, ως⟩ εγκρα/τιστάς ⟨τε⟩ είναι και
αοργήτους. θανάτου δε καταφρονουσι, χαίροντες ηνίκα μετά
συνειδήσεως αγαθ(ης) (τ)ε(λ)ευτωσιν. ει δε και αικίζοιτό τις των
τοιούτων, (ίν)α η τον νόμον δυσφημήση η ειδωλόθυτον φάγη, ου
π(οι)ήσει, υπομένων θανειν και βασάνους βαστά(σ)αι, ίνα το
συνειδός μη παρέλθη.

---

[12] The mss. do not have του θεου, which is inserted here by Marcovich from *War* 2. 148, with additional support in Porphyry and the Slavonic text of Eusebius.

in the first instance give those who come forward to gain admission as disciples), and cover it on all sides with their garment as they sit, asserting that they should not insult the rays of the god.[12] They then replace the upturned soil into the pit. For doing this they choose the more lonely spots. But after they have performed this operation, immediately they undergo ablution, as if the excrement pollutes them.

They have in the lapse of time undergone divisions, and they do not preserve their system of training after a similar manner, for they have been split up into four parties.[13] For some of them discipline themselves more than is requisite, so that they would not handle even a current coin, saying that they ought not either to carry, or behold, or fashion an image; wherefore no one of those goes into a city, lest he should enter through a gate at which statues are erected, regarding it a violation of law to pass beneath images. Another group, if they happen to hear any one maintaining a discussion concerning God and His laws—supposing he is an uncircumcised person, one of them will closely watch such a man until he catches him in any place alone, when he will threaten to slay him if he refuses to undergo the rite of circumcision, and if the latter is not willing to comply with this request, he spares not, but even kills him. It is from this occurrence that they have also received their appellation, being denominated Zealots, or, by others, Sicarii. Others call no one Lord except the Deity, even though one of them should be put to torture or even killed. Those of the later period have to such an extent declined in their practices that those who continue in the original customs would not even touch them—if they happen to come in contact with them, they immediately resort to ablution, as if they had touched one belonging to an alien tribe.

They are also in most cases of so great longevity as even to live longer than a hundred years. They assert that this derives both from their extreme devotion to religion, and their condemnation of all excess in their mode of life, and from their being temperate and incapable of anger. They despise death, rejoicing when they can die with a good conscience. If one of such men is even put to the torture to induce him either to speak evil of the law or to eat what is offered in sacrifice to an idol, he will not do it, submitting to death and enduring torment rather than violate his conscience.

---

[13] Nothing in the rest of this paragraph is found in *War* 2. 150 ff. The groups to which Hippolytus refers are described by Josephus in similar terms elsewhere in his writings, but there they are not considered as Essenes.

27 Έρρωται δε παρ' αυτοίς και ο της αναστάσεως λόγος· ομολογούσι γαρ και την σάρκα αναστήσεσθαι και έσεσθαι αθάνατον, ον τρόπον ήδη αθάνατός εστιν η ψυχή. ην χωρισθείσαν ⟨του σώματος⟩ νυν [εστιν] εις ένα χώρον εύπνουν και φωτεινόν ⟨αναφέρεσθαι και εκεί⟩ αναπαύεσθαι έως κρίσεως· ον χώρον Έλληνες ⟨τούτων⟩ ακούσαντες μακάρων νήσους ωνόμασαν. — αλλά και έτερα τούτων δόγματα πολλ⟨α⟩ οι των Ελλήνων ⟨σοφοί⟩ σφετερισάμενοι ιδίας δόξας συνεστήσαντο· έστι γαρ η κατά τούτους άσκησις περί το θείον αρχαιοτέρα πάντων εθνών, ως δείκνυσθαι πάντας τους περί θεού ειπείν τετολμηκότας ή περί της των όντων δημιουργίας μη ετέρωθεν παρειληφέναι τας αρχάς ή από της Ιουδαϊκής νομοθεσίας. ων μάλιστα Πυθαγόρας και οι από της Στοάς παρ' Αιγυπτίοις τούτοις μαθητευθέντες ⟨τας αρχάς⟩ παρέλαβον· λέγουσι γαρ και κρίσιν έσεσθαι, και του παντός εκπύρωσιν, και τους αδίκους κολασθήσεσθαι εις αεί. —ασκείται δε εν αυτοίς ⟨και⟩ το προφητεύειν και προλέγειν τα εσόμενα.

28 (Ε)στι μεν ουν και έτερον Εσ⟨σ⟩ηνών τάγμα· ⟨οι⟩ τοις μεν αυτοίς ήθεσι και διαίτη χρώμενοι, ενί δε τούτων ενδιαλ⟨λ⟩ά(ττ)ουσι, [(τ)ου(s)] (τ)ω γαμείν, δεινόν τι λέγοντες δραν τους α⟨πο⟩ποιήσα(ντα)s / γάμον· προς ⟨γαρ⟩ την αναίρεσιν του βίου γίνεσθαι τούτο και μη δείν εκκόπτειν την των τέκ(νω)ν διαδοχήν φάσκοντες, ως ει πάντες τούτο φρονήσειαν, εκκοπήσεσθαι ραδίως το παν γένος ανθρώπων. δοκιμάζουσι μέντοι τρι(ε)τία τας γαμετάς· επάν δε τρις καθαρθώσιν εις (πείρα)ν το(υ) δύνασθαι τίκτειν, ούτως άγονται. ταις ⟨δ'⟩ εγκύμοσιν ουχ ομιλούσιν, επιδεικνύμενοι το μη δι' ηδονήν γαμείν, αλλά δια τέκνων χρείαν. ομοίως δε και αι γυναίκες απολούονται, και αυταί επέν⟨δυμ⟩α ενδυόμεναι λινούν, ον τρόπον οι άνδρες τα περιζώματα. ταύτα μεν ουν ⟨τα⟩ κατά Εσ⟨σ⟩ηνούς ⟨έθη⟩.

---

[14] Contrast *War* 2. 154–5.
[15] Contrast *War* 2. 155.

The doctrine of the resurrection has also derived support among 27 them, for they acknowledge both that the flesh will rise again, and that it will be immortal,[14] in the same manner as the soul is already imperishable. They maintain that when the soul has been separated from the body, it is now borne into one place, which is well ventilated and full of light, and there it rests until judgement.[15] This locality the Greeks were acquainted with by hearsay, calling it Isles of the Blessed. But there are many other tenets of these men which the wise of the Greeks have appropriated and thus have from time to time formed their own opinions. For the discipline of these men in regard to the Divinity is of greater antiquity than that of all nations. So it is that the proof is at hand that all those who have ventured to make assertions concerning God, or concerning the creation of existing things, derived their principles from no other source than from Jewish legislation. Among these, Pythagoras especially and the Stoics[16] among the Egyptians derived their principles after becoming disciples of these men, for they affirm that there will be both a judgement and a conflagration of the universe, and that the wicked will be eternally punished. ⌈And among them is cultivated also the practice of prophecy and the prediction of future events.⌉

There is then another order of the Essenes who use the same customs 28 and prescribed method of living but make an alteration from these in one respect, which is marriage. They maintain that those who have abrogated matrimony are doing something terrible since this behaviour leads to the destruction of life, and they assert that one ought not to cut off the succession of children, since, if all entertained this opinion, the entire race of men[17] would easily be exterminated. However, they make a trial of their betrothed women for a period of three years; and when they have been three times purified, with a view of testing their ability of bringing forth children, so they wed then. They do not, however, cohabit with pregnant women, showing that they marry not from sensual motives, but for the advantage of having children. The women undergo ablution in a similar manner and are themselves also arrayed in a linen garment, after the mode in which the men wear their girdles. These, then, are the customs according to the Essenes.

---

[16] Cf. *Ant.* 15. 371; *Life* 12.
[17] Contrast *War* 2. 160.

APPENDIX

Philo, *On the Contemplative Life*, 1–2, 11–40, 63–90

The bulk of this treatise (i.e. the sections included below) consists in a favourable description of the Jewish religious community of the Therapeutae, whose practices are contrasted to the less moral behaviour current in ordinary society. The authenticity of the work was doubted in the past primarily because the customs of the sect seemed too similar to those of Christian monks and a Christian forger was suspected; it is indeed striking that Eusebius in the early fourth century believed that Philo was referring to Christians (*Eccl. Hist.* 2. 17). It may also be noted that Philo does not show knowledge of Therapeutae elsewhere in his works even though it would have been very appropriate to mention them in various places in connection with his general advocacy of the contemplative life, and that the parody of Plato's *Symposium* in sections 59–62 is strange for an avowed admirer of Plato. However, the language, style and range of ideas are all compatible with Philo's writings elsewhere and the work is now generally regarded as genuine.

The treatise was intended to stress universal ethical teachings and there is a clear danger that the life of the Therapeutae may have been idealised. It is indeed hard to see what was their source of livelihood if they abstained so consistently from work.

On the possible relationship between Therapeutae and Essenes, see the Introduction, pp. 16–17.

The translation is that of F. C. Conybeare (1895), somewhat emended.

1 Ἐσσαίων πέρι διαλεχθείς, οἳ τὸν πρακτικὸν ἐζήλωσαν καὶ διεπόνησαν βίον ἐν ἅπασιν ἢ—τὸ γοῦν φορητότερον εἰπεῖν—τοῖς πλείστοις μέρεσι διενεγκόντες, αὐτίκα καὶ περὶ τῶν θεωρίαν ἀσπασαμένων ἀκολουθίᾳ τῆς πραγματείας ἑπόμενος τὰ προσήκοντα λέξω, μηδὲν οἴκοθεν ἕνεκα τοῦ βελτιῶσαι προστιθείς, ὃ δρᾶν ἔθος ἐν σπάνει καλῶν ἐπιτηδευμάτων ἅπασι τοῖς ποιηταῖς καὶ λογογράφοις, ἀλλ' ἀτεχνῶς αὐτῆς περιεχόμενος τῆς ἀληθείας, πρὸς ἣν οἶδ' ὅτι καὶ ὁ δεινότατος εἰπεῖν ἀπαγορεύσει. διαθλητέον δὲ ὅμως καὶ διαγωνιστέον· οὐ γὰρ δεῖ τὸ μέγεθος τῆς τῶν ἀνδρῶν ἀρετῆς αἴτιον ἀφωνίας γενέσθαι τοῖς μηδὲν καλὸν ἡσυχάζεσθαι
2 δικαιοῦσιν. ἡ δὲ προαίρεσις τῶν φιλοσόφων εὐθὺς ἐμφαίνεται διὰ τῆς προσρήσεως· θεραπευταὶ γὰρ καὶ θεραπευτρίδες ἐτύμως καλοῦνται, ἤτοι παρόσον ἰατρικὴν ἐπαγγέλλονται κρείσσονα τῆς κατὰ πόλεις—ἡ μὲν γὰρ σώματα θεραπεύει μόνον, ἐκείνη δὲ καὶ ψυχὰς νόσοις κεκρατημένας χαλεπαῖς τε καὶ δυσιάτοις, ἃς ἐγκατέσκηψαν ἡδοναὶ καὶ ἐπιθυμίαι καὶ λῦπαι καὶ φόβοι πλεονεξίαι τε καὶ ἀφροσύναι καὶ ἀδικίαι καὶ τὸ τῶν ἄλλων παθῶν καὶ κακιῶν ἀνήνυτον πλῆθος—ἢ παρόσον ἐκ φύσεως καὶ τῶν ἱερῶν νόμων ἐπαιδεύθησαν θεραπεύειν τὸ ὄν, ὃ καὶ ἀγαθοῦ κρεῖττόν ἐστι καὶ ἑνὸς εἰλικρινέστερον καὶ μονάδος ἀρχεγονώτερον.

* * * * *

[1] This could mean either that the Therapeutae were a contemplative sort of Essene or that they were a different group altogether.

Appendix

I have now spoken of the Essenes who followed with zeal and constant diligence the life of Action, and so excelled in all, or, to put it more moderately, in most particulars. And therefore I will presently, following the due sequence of my treatise, say whatever is meet to be said about them that have embraced contemplation,[1] though without adding aught out of my own mind in order to exalt them unduly, as are wont to do all the poets and composers of tales in their dearth of noble examples. But I adhere simply to the bare truth, before which I know well even the most eloquent tongue will be weak and fail. Yet must I face the struggle and strive to master the task. For the greatness of these men's excellency must not be a cause of dumbness to them that hold that nothing noble should be hidden in silence. But the purpose and will of the lovers of wisdom is discovered in their very name and title; for they are most fitly called healers, male and female.[2] Either by reason of their professing an art of healing more excellent than that which is found in cities—for this heals men's bodies alone, but that their souls also, when overcome by diseases difficult and hard to heal, souls smitten and undone by pleasures and lusts and sorrows and fears, by forms of avarice and folly and injustice, and all the countless swarm of passions and vices: for this reason, or because they have been educated by nature and the holy laws to worship the true Being, which is more excellent than the good, and simpler than the unit, and more primitive than the Monad.

* * * * *

Then follows a description of various kinds of paganism, from the philosophical to the crude. All such forms of worship are declared to be inferior to that of the Therapeutae.

* * * * *

---

[2] Literally: 'Therapeutae and Therapeutidae'. Compare the notion of healing in the name to the name of the Essenes (see Introduction, p. 2). See *War* 2. 136. On women, see below, sect. 32.

11 Τὸ δὲ θεραπευτικὸν γένος βλέπειν ἀεὶ προδιδασκόμενον τῆς τοῦ ὄντος θέας ἐφιέσθω καὶ τὸν αἰσθητὸν ἥλιον ὑπερβαινέτω καὶ μηδέποτε τὴν τάξιν ταύτην λειπέτω πρὸς τελείαν ἄγουσαν εὐ-
12 δαιμονίαν. οἱ δὲ ἐπὶ θεραπείαν ἰόντες οὔτε ἐξ ἔθους οὔτε ἐκ παραινέσεως ἢ παρακλήσεώς τινων, ἀλλ' ὑπ' ἔρωτος ἁρπασθέντες οὐρανίου, καθάπερ οἱ βακχευόμενοι καὶ κορυβαντιῶντες ἐνθουσιάζουσι, μέχρις ἂν τὸ ποθούμενον ἴδωσιν.
13 Εἶτα διὰ τὸν τῆς ἀθανάτου καὶ μακαρίας ζωῆς ἵμερον τετελευτηκέναι νομίζοντες ἤδη τὸν θνητὸν βίον ἀπολείπουσι τὰς οὐσίας υἱοῖς ἢ θυγατράσιν εἴτε καὶ ἄλλοις συγγενέσιν, ἑκουσίῳ γνώμῃ προκληρονομούμενοι, οἷς δὲ μὴ συγγενεῖς εἰσιν, ἑταίροις καὶ φίλοις· ἔδει γὰρ τοὺς τὸν βλέποντα πλοῦτον ἐξ ἑτοίμου λαβόντας τὸν τυφλὸν
14 παραχωρῆσαι τοῖς ἔτι τὰς διανοίας τυφλώττουσιν. Ἀναξαγόραν καὶ Δημόκριτον Ἕλληνες ᾄδουσιν, ὅτι φιλοσοφίας ἱμέρῳ πληχθέντες μηλοβότους εἴασαν γενέσθαι τὰς οὐσίας· ἄγαμαι τοὺς ἄνδρας καὶ αὐτὸς γενομένους χρημάτων κρείττονας. ἀλλὰ πόσῳ βελτίονες οἱ μὴ θρέμμασιν ἐμβόσκεσθαι τὰς κτήσεις ἀνέντες, ἀλλὰ τὰς ἀνθρώπων ἐνδείας, συγγενῶν ἢ φίλων, ἐπανορθωσάμενοι καὶ ἐξ ἀπόρων εὐπόρους ἀποφήναντες; ἐκεῖνο μὲν γὰρ ἀπερίσκεπτον—ἵνα μὴ μανιῶδες ἐπ' ἀνδρῶν, οὓς ἡ Ἑλλὰς ἐθαύμασεν, εἴπω τὸ ἔργον—, τοῦτο δὲ νηφάλιον καὶ μετὰ φρονήσεως ἠκριβωμένον
15 περιττῆς. οἱ πολέμιοι τί πλέον δρῶσιν ἢ κείρουσι καὶ δενδροτομοῦσι τὴν τῶν ἀντιπάλων χώραν, ἵνα σπάνει τῶν ἀναγκαίων πιεσθέντες ἐνδῶσι; τοῦτο οἱ περὶ Δημόκριτον τοῖς ἀφ' αἵματος εἰργάσαντο χειροποίητον ἔνδειαν καὶ πενίαν αὑτοῖς κατασκευάσαντες, οὐκ ἐξ ἐπιβουλῆς ἴσως, ἀλλὰ τῷ μὴ προϊδέσθαι καὶ
16 περιαθρῆσαι τὸ τοῖς ἄλλοις συμφέρον. πόσῳ δὴ κρείττους οὗτοι καὶ θαυμασιώτεροι, χρησάμενοι μὲν οὐκ ἐλάττοσι ταῖς πρὸς φιλοσοφίαν ὁρμαῖς, μεγαλόνοιαν δὲ ὀλιγωρίας προτιμήσαντες καὶ χαρισάμενοι τὰς οὐσίας, ἀλλὰ μὴ διαφθείραντες, ἵνα καὶ ἑτέρους καὶ ἑαυτοὺς ὠφελήσωσι, τοὺς μὲν ἐν ἀφθόνοις περιουσίαις, ἑαυτοὺς δὲ ἐν τῷ φιλοσοφεῖν; αἱ γὰρ χρημάτων καὶ κτημάτων ἐπιμέλειαι τοὺς χρόνους ἀναλίσκουσι· χρόνου δὲ φείδεσθαι καλόν,

But, on the other hand, let the Therapeutic kind, that hath not only the eye, but is ever learning beside to see with it, aspire to a vision of the true Being; let it even soar above the sun which our senses behold, and never forsake this post which leads to perfect happiness. But those who draw nigh unto therapy do so not from custom, nor from advice, or exhortations of any; but because they are rapt by heavenly love, like Bacchants or Corybantic revellers, and are lost in ecstasy until they behold the desire of their souls.

But then, out of their yearning after the immortal and blessed life, they esteem their mortal life to have already ended, and so leave their possessions to their sons or daughters, or, in default of them, to other kinsmen, of their own free will leaving to these their heritage in advance; but, if they have no kinsmen, to their comrades and friends. For it needs must be that they who have received the wealth which sees from a free and open store, should resign the wealth which is blind to those whose minds are still blinded. The Greeks sing the praises of Anaxagoras and Democritus, because, smitten with the desire for wisdom, they gave up their properties to be sheep-runs. I, too, admire these men for having risen superior to wealth. Yet how much better are those who, instead of abandoning their possessions for the beasts to batten upon, ministered to the wants of human beings, kinsmen or friends, aiding them in their need, and raising them from helpless poverty into affluence! For, indeed, their much-praised action was ill-considered, not to use the word 'mad', of men whom Greece admired. But the conduct of these is sober, and exhibits the perfection proper to the highest wisdom. What worse acts do one's country's enemies commit than to cut down the crops and hew down the trees of those with whom they are at war, in order that a scarcity of the necessaries of life may weigh hard on them and compel them to give in? Yet this is what men like Democritus did to their own blood-relations, inventing an artificial want and hunger for them; not, it may be, of malice prepense, but because they did not look round them and have an eye to foresee what was for the benefit of their fellows. How much superior, then, and more admirable are these men whom I describe! whose enthusiasm for Philosophy was no whit less than theirs, while at the same time they preferred to be magnanimous to being contemptuous and neglectful; and so freely gave away their properties instead of letting them go to ruin, in order, by so doing, to advantage others as well as themselves—others, by surrounding them with plenty; themselves, by their devotion to philosophy. For the cares of wealth and chattels consume the users thereof; but it is well to husband our time,

ἐπειδὴ κατὰ τὸν ἰατρὸν Ἱπποκράτην »ὁ μὲν βίος βραχύς, ἡ δὲ
17 τέχνη μακρή«. τοῦτό μοι δοκεῖ καὶ Ὅμηρος αἰνίξασθαι ἐν Ἰλιάδι
κατὰ τὴν ἀρχὴν τῆς τρισκαιδεκάτης ῥαψῳδίας διὰ τούτων τῶν
ἐπῶν·

»Μυσῶν τ᾽ ἀγχεμάχων καὶ ἀγαυῶν Ἱππημολγῶν,
γλακτοφάγων ἀβίων τε, δικαιοτάτων ἀνθρώπων«,

ὡς τῆς μὲν περὶ βίον σπουδῆς καὶ χρηματισμὸν ἀδικίαν γεννώσης
διὰ τὸ ἄνισον, δικαιοσύνην δὲ τῆς ἐναντίας προαιρέσεως ἕνεκα
ἰσότητος, καθ᾽ ἣν ὁ τῆς φύσεως πλοῦτος ὥρισται καὶ παρευημερεῖ
τὸν ἐν ταῖς κεναῖς δόξαις.

18 Ὅταν οὖν ἐκστῶσι τῶν οὐσιῶν, ὑπ᾽ οὐδενὸς ἔτι δελεαζόμενοι
φεύγουσιν ἀμεταστρεπτὶ καταλιπόντες ἀδελφούς, τέκνα, γυναῖκας,
γονεῖς, πολυανθρώπους συγγενείας, φιλικὰς ἑταιρείας, τὰς πα-
τρίδας, ἐν αἷς ἐγεννήθησαν καὶ ἐτράφησαν, ἐπειδὴ τὸ σύνηθες
19 ὁλκὸν καὶ δελεάσαι δυνατώτατον. μετοικίζονται δὲ οὐκ εἰς ἑτέραν
πόλιν, ὥσπερ οἱ πρᾶσιν αἰτούμενοι παρὰ τῶν κεκτημένων ἀτυχεῖς
ἢ κακόδουλοι δεσποτῶν ὑπαλλαγήν, οὐκ ἐλευθερίαν, αὑτοῖς
ἐκπορίζοντες—πᾶσα γὰρ πόλις, καὶ ἡ εὐνομωτάτη, γέμει θορύβων
20 καὶ ταραχῶν ἀμυθήτων, ἃς οὐκ ἂν ὑπομεῖναι τις ἅπαξ ὑπὸ σοφίας
ἀχθείς—, ἀλλὰ τειχῶν ἔξω ποιοῦνται τὰς διατριβὰς ἐν κήποις ἢ
μοναγρίαις ἐρημίαν μεταδιώκοντες, οὐ διά τινα ὠμὴν ἐπιτετηδευ-
μένην μισανθρωπίαν, ἀλλὰ τὰς ἐκ τῶν ἀνομοίων τὸ ἦθος ἐπιμιξίας
ἀλυσιτελεῖς καὶ βλαβερὰς εἰδότες.

21 Πολλαχοῦ μὲν οὖν τῆς οἰκουμένης ἐστὶ τὸ γένος—ἔδει γὰρ
ἀγαθοῦ τελείου μετασχεῖν καὶ τὴν Ἑλλάδα καὶ τὴν βάρβαρον—,
πλεονάζει δὲ ἐν Αἰγύπτῳ καθ᾽ ἕκαστον τῶν ἐπικαλουμένων νόμων
22 καὶ μάλιστα περὶ τὴν Ἀλεξάνδρειαν. οἱ δὲ πανταχόθεν ἄριστοι
καθάπερ εἰς πατρίδα {θεραπευτῶν} ἀποικίαν στέλλονται πρός τι
χωρίον ἐπιτηδειότατον, ὅπερ ἐστὶν ὑπὲρ λίμνης Μαρείας κείμενον
ἐπὶ γεωλόφου χθαμαλωτέρου, σφόδρα εὐκαίρως, ἀσφαλείας τε
23 ἕνεκα καὶ ἀέρος εὐκρασίας. τὴν μὲν οὖν ἀσφάλειαν αἱ ἐν κύκλῳ
παρέχουσιν ἐπαύλεις τε καὶ κῶμαι, τὴν δὲ περὶ τὸν ἀέρα εὐκρασίαν

---

[3] For avoidance of cities, see *Q.o.p.* 76.

since, as the physician Hippocrates saith, 'Life is short, but art is long.' And methinks this, too, is what Homer hinted at in the Iliad, at the beginning of the thirteenth rhapsody, in these words:

> Of the Masi, fighting hand-to-hand, and of the high-born mare-milkers,
> That live on milk, and are simple in life—most just men.

He means that anxiety about life and money-making begets injustice by the inequality it produces, whereas the opposite motive begets justice through equality. And it is in accordance with such equality that the wealth of nature has its limits assigned, and excels that which consists in vainglory and empty fancies.

So soon, then, as they have divested themselves of their properties, without allowing anything to further ensnare them, they flee without turning back, having abandoned brethren, children, wives, parents, all the throng of their kindred, all their friendships with companions, yea, their countries in which they were born and bred. For, in truth, what we are familiar with has an attractive force, and is the most powerful of baits. However, they do not go away to live in another city; like those who claim of their owners to be sold, unhappy wights or naughty slaves, and who so win for themselves, not freedom, but a mere change of masters. For every city, even the best governed, teems with riots and troubles untold, which no one would endure that had once let himself be led by wisdom. Rather do they make for themselves their settlements outside the walls, in gardens or solitary cots, seeking solitude, not from any harsh and deliberate hatred of mankind, but as knowing that the intercourse with and the influence of those unlike themselves in character cannot profit, but only harm them.[3]

Now this kind is to be found in many parts of the world; for it is right that the Greeks, as well as Barbarians, should have their portion in the perfect good. But it is very numerous in Egypt in each of the so-called Nomes, and most of all in the neighbourhood of Alexandria. And the best people from all parts, as if they were going to the native country of the Therapeutae, leave their homes and emigrate to a certain spot most suitable, which is situated above the Mareotic lake, upon a low hill, very conveniently placed both for its security and well-tempered climate.[4] The requisite security is afforded by the hamlets and villages which lie all around; and the well-tempered climate by the breezes given off

---

[4] Compare, for Essenes as (exclusively?) from Palestine, *Q.o.p.* 75.

αἱ ἔκ τε τῆς λίμνης ἀνεστομωμένης εἰς τὴν θάλατταν καὶ τοῦ πελάγους ἐγγὺς ὄντος ἀναδιδόμεναι συνεχεῖς αὖραι, λεπταὶ μὲν αἱ ἐκ τοῦ πελάγους, παχεῖαι δὲ αἱ ἀπὸ τῆς λίμνης, ὧν ἡ μῖξις ὑγιεινοτάτην κατάστασιν ἀπεργάζεται.

24 Αἱ δὲ οἰκίαι τῶν συνεληλυθότων σφόδρα μὲν εὐτελεῖς εἰσι, πρὸς δύο τὰ ἀναγκαιότατα σκέπην παρέχουσαι, πρός τε τὸν ἀφ' ἡλίου φλογμὸν καὶ τὸν ἀπ' ἀέρος κρυμόν· οὔτε δὲ ἐγγύς, ὥσπερ αἱ ἐν τοῖς ἄστεσιν, —ὀχληρὸν γὰρ καὶ δυσάρεστον τοῖς ἐρημίαν ἐζηλωκόσι καὶ μεταδιώκουσιν αἱ γειτνιάσεις—οὔτε πόρρω, δι' ἣν ἀσπάζονται κοινωνίαν καὶ ἵνα, εἰ λῃστῶν γένοιτο ἔφοδος, ἀλλήλοις ἐπιβοηθῶ-
25 σιν. ἐν ἑκάστῃ δέ ἐστιν οἴκημα ἱερόν, ὃ καλεῖται σεμνεῖον καὶ μοναστήριον, ἐν ᾧ μονούμενοι τὰ τοῦ σεμνοῦ βίου μυστήρια τελοῦνται, μηδὲν εἰσκομίζοντες, μὴ ποτόν, μὴ σιτίον, μηδέ τι τῶν ἄλλων ὅσα πρὸς τὰς τοῦ σώματος χρείας ἀναγκαῖα, ἀλλὰ νόμους καὶ λόγια θεσπισθέντα διὰ προφητῶν καὶ ὕμνους καὶ τὰ ἄλλα οἷς
26 ἐπιστήμη καὶ εὐσέβεια συναύξονται καὶ τελειοῦνται. ἀεὶ μὲν οὖν ἄληστον ἔχουσι τὴν τοῦ θεοῦ μνήμην, ὡς καὶ δι' ὀνειράτων μηδὲν ἕτερον ἢ τὰ κάλλη τῶν θείων ἀρετῶν καὶ δυνάμεων φαντασιοῦ-σθαι· πολλοὶ γοῦν καὶ ἐκλαλοῦσιν ἐν ὕπνοις ὀνειροπολούμενοι τὰ
27 τῆς ἱερᾶς φιλοσοφίας ἀοίδιμα δόγματα. δὶς δὲ καθ' ἑκάστην ἡμέραν εἰώθασιν εὔχεσθαι, περὶ τὴν ἕω καὶ περὶ τὴν ἑσπέραν, ἡλίου μὲν ἀνίσχοντος εὐημερίαν αἰτούμενοι τὴν ὄντως εὐημερίαν, φωτὸς οὐρανίου τὴν διάνοιαν αὐτῶν ἀναπλησθῆναι, δυομένου δὲ ὑπὲρ τοῦ τὴν ψυχὴν τοῦ τῶν αἰσθήσεων καὶ αἰσθητῶν ὄχλου παντελῶς ἐπικουφισθεῖσαν, ἐν τῷ ἑαυτῆς συνεδρίῳ καὶ βουλευτη-
28 ρίῳ γενομένην, ἀλήθειαν ἰχνηλατεῖν. τὸ δὲ ἐξ ἑωθινοῦ μέχρις ἑσπέρας διάστημα σύμπαν αὐτοῖς ἐστιν ἄσκησις· ἐντυγχάνοντες γὰρ τοῖς ἱεροῖς γράμμασι φιλοσοφοῦσι τὴν πάτριον φιλοσοφίαν ἀλληγοροῦντες, ἐπειδὴ σύμβολα τὰ τῆς ῥητῆς ἑρμηνείας νομίζου-σιν ἀποκεκρυμμένης φύσεως ἐν ὑπονοίαις δηλουμένης.
29 Ἔστι δὲ αὐτοῖς καὶ συγγράμματα παλαιῶν ἀνδρῶν, οἳ τῆς αἱρέσεως ἀρχηγέται γενόμενοι πολλὰ μνημεῖα τῆς ἐν τοῖς ἀλληγορουμένοις ἰδέας ἀπέλιπον, οἷς καθάπερ τισὶν ἀρχετύποις

---

[5] On self-defence, cf. *War* 2. 125.
[6] On prophecy, see *War* 2. 159. But is this the same phenomenon?

without ceasing, both from the lake debouching into the sea, and from the sea in close proximity. The sea-breezes are light, and those which blow from the lake are heavy, but blended they produce a most healthy condition of atmosphere.

And the dwellings of those thus met together are indeed of a cheap and simple kind, affording protection against the two things which most require it, namely, the extreme heat of the sun and the chilly cold of the air. For they are neither too close to one another, as in towns; since close proximity would be burdensome and ill-pleasing to those who are seeking to satisfy their desire for solitude; nor, on the other hand, are they far apart, lest they forfeit the communion which they prize and the power of aiding each other in case of an attack of robbers.[5] But in each house there is a holy room, which is called the sanctuary and monastery; because in it they celebrate all alone the mysteries of the holy life, bringing into it nothing, neither drink, nor food, nor any other of the things necessary unto the wants of the body; but only the law and the oracles delivered under inspiration by the prophets along with the Psalms, and the other [books] by means of which religion and sound knowledge grow together into one perfect whole. And so it is that they for ever remember God and forget him not; in such wise that even in their dreams they picture to themselves nothing else but the beauties of the divine excellencies and powers. Yea, and many of them even utter forth in their sleep, when lapt in dreams, the glorious doctrines of their holy philosophy.[6] And twice every day they are accustomed to pray, about dawn and about eventide; praying at sunrise for a fair day for themselves,[7] for the day, which is really fair, which meaneth that their minds be filled with heavenly light. But at sunset they pray that the soul be wholly relieved of the disorderly throng of the senses and of sensible things, and left free to track out and explore truth in its own conclave and council-chamber. But the entire interval from dawn to evening is given up by them to spiritual exercises. For they read the holy scriptures and draw out in thought and allegory their ancestral philosophy. Since they regard the literal meanings as symbols of an inner and hidden nature revealing itself in covert ideas.[8]

But they have also writings drawn up by the men of a former age, who were the founders of their sect, and left many memorials of the form used in allegorical interpretation; and these writings they use as

---

[7] Cf. *War* 2. 128; below, sect. 89.
[8] For allegory as typical of Therapeutae, see *Q.o.p.* 82 on Essenes.

χρώμενοι μιμοῦνται τῆς προαιρέσεως τὸν τρόπον· ὥστε οὐ θεωροῦσι μόνον, ἀλλὰ καὶ ποιοῦσιν ᾄσματα καὶ ὕμνους εἰς τὸν θεὸν διὰ παντοίων μέτρων καὶ μελῶν, ἃ ῥυθμοῖς σεμνοτέροις ἀναγκαίως χαράττουσι.

30 Τὰς μὲν οὖν ἐξ ἡμέρας χωρὶς ἕκαστοι μονούμενοι παρ' ἑαυτοῖς ἐν τοῖς λεχθεῖσι μοναστηρίοις φιλοσοφοῦσι, τὴν αὔλειον οὐχ ὑπερβαίνοντες, ἀλλ' οὐδὲ ἐξ ἀπόπτου θεωροῦντες· ταῖς δὲ ἑβδόμαις συνέρχονται καθάπερ εἰς κοινὸν σύλλογον καὶ καθ' ἡλικίαν ἑξῆς καθέζονται μετὰ τοῦ πρέποντος σχήματος, εἴσω τὰς χεῖρας ἔχοντες, τὴν μὲν δεξιὰν μεταξὺ στέρνου καὶ γενείου, τὴν δὲ
31 εὐώνυμον ὑπεσταλμένην παρὰ τῇ λαγόνι. παρελθὼν δὲ ὁ πρεσβύτατος καὶ τῶν δογμάτων ἐμπειρότατος διαλέγεται, καθεστῶτι μὲν τῷ βλέμματι, καθεστώσῃ δὲ τῇ φωνῇ, μετὰ λογισμοῦ καὶ φρονήσεως, οὐ δεινότητα λόγων ὥσπερ οἱ ῥήτορες ἢ οἱ νῦν σοφισταὶ παρεπιδεικνύμενος, ἀλλὰ τὴν ἐν τοῖς νοήμασι διηρευνηκὼς καὶ διερμηνεύων ἀκρίβειαν, ἥτις οὐκ ἄκροις ὠσὶν ἐφιζάνει, ἀλλὰ δι' ἀκοῆς ἐπὶ ψυχὴν ἔρχεται καὶ βεβαίως ἐπιμένει. καθ' ἡσυχίαν δὲ οἱ ἄλλοι πάντες ἀκροῶνται, τὸν ἔπαινον νεύμασιν ὄψεως ἢ κεφαλῆς παραδηλοῦντες αὐτὸ μόνον.
32 Τὸ δὲ κοινὸν τοῦτο σεμνεῖον, εἰς ὃ ταῖς ἑβδόμαις συνέρχονται, διπλοῦς ἐστι περίβολος, ὁ μὲν εἰς ἀνδρῶνα, ὁ δὲ εἰς γυναικωνῖτιν ἀποκριθείς· καὶ γὰρ καὶ γυναῖκες ἐξ ἔθους συνακροῶνται τὸν αὐτὸν
33 ζῆλον καὶ τὴν αὐτὴν προαίρεσιν ἔχουσαι. ὁ δὲ μεταξὺ τῶν οἴκων τοῖχος τὸ μὲν ἐξ ἐδάφους ἐπὶ τρεῖς ἢ τέσσαρας πήχεις εἰς τὸ ἄνω συνῳκοδόμηται θωρακίου τρόπον, τὸ δὲ ἄχρι τέγους ἀνάγειον ἀχανὲς ἀνεῖται, δυοῖν ἕνεκα, τοῦ τε τὴν πρέπουσαν αἰδῶ τῇ γυναικείᾳ φύσει διατηρεῖσθαι καὶ τοῦ τὴν ἀντίληψιν ἔχειν εὐμαρῆ καθεζομένας ἐν ἐπηκόῳ, μηδενὸς τὴν τοῦ διαλεγομένου φωνὴν ἐμποδίζοντος.
34 Ἐγκράτειαν δὲ ὥσπερ τινὰ θεμέλιον προκαταβαλλόμενοι τῆς ψυχῆς τὰς ἄλλας ἐποικοδομοῦσιν ἀρετάς. σιτίον ἢ ποτὸν οὐδεὶς ἂν αὐτῶν προσενέγκαιτο πρὸ ἡλίου δύσεως, ἐπεὶ τὸ μὲν φιλοσοφεῖν ἄξιον φωτὸς κρίνουσιν εἶναι, σκότους δὲ τὰς τοῦ σώματος

---

[9] For sectarian literature, see *War* 2. 142.
[10] Contrast to this isolation *War* 2. 129 etc. on communal life of Essenes.
[11] Compare this combined sanctuary and refectory (see below, sect. 66 ff.) to the dining hall at Qumran.

exemplars of a kind, emulating the ideal of character traced out in them.⁹ And so it is that they do not only contemplate, but also compose songs and hymns to God in divers strains and measures, which they write out in solemn rhythms as best they can.

Now during the six days they remain apart, in strict isolation one from the other,¹⁰ in their houses in the monasteries afore mentioned; never passing the courtyard gate, nay, not even surveying it from a distance. But every seventh day they come together, as it were, into a common assembly; and sit down in order according to age in the becoming posture; holding their hands inwards, the right hand between the chest and the chin, but the left tucked down along the flank. And then the one that is eldest and most skilled in their principles discourses, with steady glance and steady voice, with argument and wisdom; not making a display of his cleverness in speaking, like the rhetors or the sophists of to-day, but having carefully sifted and carefully interpreting the exact meaning of the thoughts, which meaning doth not merely alight on the outer ear, but passes through their organs of hearing into the soul, and there firmly abides. But the others all listen, in silence, merely hinting their approval by an inclination of eye or head.

And this common sanctuary,¹¹ in which they meet on the seventh days, is a double enclosure, divided into one chamber for the men and another for the women. For women, too, as well as men, of custom form part of the audience, having the same zeal and following the same mode of life.¹² But the wall which runs midway up the buildings is, part of it, built up together like a breastwork from the floor to a height of three or four cubits; but that part which extends above up to the roof is left open for two reasons: namely, to safeguard the modesty which is proper to woman's nature, and, at the same time, to facilitate on the part of those who sit within the auditory the apprehension of what is said; there being nothing to impede the voice of him that discourses from passing freely to them.

But continence they lay down, as it were, as a primitive foundation of the soul, and on it they build up the rest of the virtues. And not one of them will partake of meat or drink before sunset;¹³ in as much as they judge the pursuit of wisdom to be consonant with the light, just as the

---

¹² There is no mention of women as sect members in any text about the Essenes.
¹³ Contrast the two daily meals of the Essenes, cf. *War* 2. 131–2.

ἀνάγκας, ὅθεν τῷ μὲν ἡμέραν, ταῖς δὲ νυκτὸς βραχύ τι μέρος ἔνειμαν. ἔνιοι δὲ καὶ διὰ τριῶν ἡμερῶν ὑπομιμνήσκονται τροφῆς, οἷς πλείων ὁ πόθος ἐπιστήμης ἐνίδρυται· τινὲς δὲ οὕτως ἐνευφραίνονται καὶ τρυφῶσιν ὑπὸ σοφίας ἑστιώμενοι πλουσίως καὶ ἀφθόνως τὰ δόγματα χορηγούσης, ὡς καὶ πρὸς διπλασίονα χρόνον ἀντέχειν καὶ μόλις δι' ἓξ ἡμερῶν ἀπογεύεσθαι τροφῆς ἀναγκαίας, ἐθισθέντες ὥσπερ φασὶ τὸ τῶν τεττίγων γένος ἀέρι τρέφεσθαι, τῆς ᾠδῆς, ὥς γε οἶμαι, τὴν ἔνδειαν ἐξευμαριζούσης. τὴν δὲ ἑβδόμην πανίερόν τινα καὶ πανέορτον εἶναι νομίζοντες ἐξαιρέτου γέρως ἠξιώκασιν, ἐν ᾗ μετὰ τὴν τῆς ψυχῆς ἐπιμέλειαν καὶ τὸ σῶμα λιπαίνουσιν, ὥσπερ ἀμέλει καὶ τὰ θρέμματα, τῶν συνεχῶν πόνων ἀνιέντες. σιτοῦνται δὲ πολυτελὲς οὐδέν, ἀλλὰ ἄρτον εὐτελῆ, καὶ ὄψον ἅλες, οὓς οἱ ἁβροδίαιτοι παραρτύουσιν ὑσσώπῳ, ποτὸν δὲ ὕδωρ ναματιαῖον αὐτοῖς ἐστιν· ἃς γὰρ ἡ φύσις ἐπέστησε τῷ θνητῷ γένει δεσποίνας, πεινάν τε καὶ δίψαν, ἀπομειλίσσονται, τῶν εἰς κολακείαν ἐπιφέροντες οὐδέν, ἀλλ' αὐτὰ τὰ χρήσιμα, ὧν ἄνευ ζῆν οὐκ ἔστι. διὰ τοῦτο ἐσθίουσι μέν, ὥστε μὴ πεινῆν, πίνουσι δέ, ὥστε μὴ διψῆν, πλησμονὴν ὡς ἐχθρόν τε καὶ ἐπίβουλον ψυχῆς τε καὶ σώματος ἐκτρεπόμενοι.

Ἐπεὶ δὲ καὶ σκέπης διττὸν εἶδος, τὸ μὲν ἐσθής, τὸ δὲ οἰκία, περὶ μὲν οἰκίας εἴρηται πρότερον, ὅτι ἐστὶν ἀκαλλώπιστος καὶ αὐτοσχέδιος, πρὸς τὸ χρειῶδες αὐτὸ μόνον εἰργασμένη· καὶ ἐσθὴς δὲ ὁμοίως εὐτελεστάτη, πρὸς ἀλέξημα κρυμοῦ τε καὶ θάλπους, χλαῖνα μὲν ἀπὸ λασίου δορᾶς παχεῖα χειμῶνος, ἐξωμὶς δὲ θέρους ἢ ὀθόνη. συνόλως γὰρ ἀσκοῦσιν ἀτυφίαν, εἰδότες τῦφον μὲν τοῦ ψεύδους ἀρχήν, ἀτυφίαν δὲ ἀληθείας, ἑκάτερον δὲ πηγῆς λόγον ἔχον· ῥέουσι γὰρ ἀπὸ μὲν τοῦ ψεύδους αἱ πολύτροποι τῶν κακῶν ἰδέαι, ἀπὸ δὲ τῆς ἀληθείας αἱ περιουσίαι τῶν ἀγαθῶν ἀνθρωπίνων τε καὶ θείων.

Βούλομαι δὲ καὶ τὰς κοινὰς συνόδους αὐτῶν καὶ ἱλαρωτέρας ἐν συμποσίοις διαγωγὰς εἰπεῖν, ἀντιτάξας τὰ τῶν ἄλλων συμπόσια. οἱ μὲν γὰρ ὅταν ἄκρατον ἐμφορήσωνται, καθάπερ οὐκ οἶνον

[14] Contrast *War* 2. 123. Colson translates 'refresh' in place of 'anoint'.

wants of the body are with the darkness. Wherefore, they assign to the former the day, but to the latter an insignificant portion of the night only. And some there are, who at the end of three days bethink themselves of food, those, namely, in whom a more profound love of knowledge is seated. But others, again, so delight and luxuriate in the banquet, in which wisdom spreads out before them in bounteous wealth her teachings, that they abstain for double that period, and barely taste of so much food as will keep them alive at the end of six days; having accustomed themselves, as they say the grasshoppers have, to live upon air; for the song of these, I suppose, assuages the feeling of want. The seventh day, however, they regard as in a manner all holy and all festal, and have therefore deemed it worthy of peculiar dignity. And on it, after due attention to the soul, they anoint[14] the body, releasing it, just as you might the lower animals, from the long spell of toil. But their diet comprises nothing expensive, but only cheap bread; and its relish is salt, which the dainty among them prepare with hyssop; and for drink they have water from a spring. For they propitiate the mistresses hunger and thirst, which nature has set over mortal creatures, offering nothing that can flatter them, but merely such useful food as life cannot be supported without. For this reason they eat only so as not to be hungry, and drink only so as not to thirst; avoiding all surfeit as dangerous and inimical to body and soul.[15]

There are then two kinds of shelter, the one consisting in the raiment, the other in the house; and we have already spoken of their houses, declaring them to be unadorned, of a rough and ready description, constructed for utility alone. But as to their raiment, it also like the house is of a very cheap kind, by way of protection only against cold and heat; being a thick cloak of shaggy hide in winter and in summer a smock without sleeves or a linen coat.[16] For they, in all respects, carry out their ideal of modest simplicity, being aware that vanity is the beginning of falsehood as simplicity is of truth; and that each is like a fountain head. For from falsehood flow the manifold forms of all evils, but from truth the wealth and fulness of blessings, both human and divine.

But it is my wish to describe their common gatherings also, and their more cheerful ways of relaxation in their banquets, contrasting therewith the banquets of the rest of the world. For others when they have

---

[15] On frugality, cf. *Q.o.p.* 77; *Apol.* 11; *War* 2. 130, 133.
[16] On summer and winter garments, cf. *Apol.* 12.

πιόντες ἀλλὰ παρακινηματικόν τι καὶ μανιῶδες καὶ εἴ τι χαλεπώτερον ἐπ' ἐκστάσει λογισμοῦ φυσικόν, ἀράσσουσι καὶ λυττῶσι τρόπον κυνῶν ἀτιθάσων καὶ ἐπανιστάμενοι δάκνουσιν ἀλλήλους καὶ ἀποτρώγουσι ῥῖνας, ὦτα, δακτύλους, ἕτερα ἄττα μέρη τοῦ σώματος, ὡς τὸν ἐπὶ Κύκλωπος καὶ τῶν Ὀδυσσέως ἑταίρων μῦθον ἀποδεδειχέναι τούτους ἀληθῆ, »ψωμούς«, ᾗ φησιν ὁ ποιητής, ἐπεσθίοντας ἀνθρώπων, καὶ ὠμότερον ἢ ἐκεῖνος.

* * * * *

63 Σιωπῶ τὰ τῶν μύθων πλάσματα καὶ τοὺς δισωμάτους, οἳ κατ' ἀρχὰς προσφύντες ἀλλήλοις ἐνωτικαῖς δυνάμεσιν αὖθις οἷα μέρη συνεληλυθότα διεζεύχθησαν, τῆς ἁρμονίας ὑφ' ἧς συνείχοντο λυθείσης· εὐπαράγωγα γὰρ ταῦτα πάντα, δυνάμενα τῇ καινότητι τῆς ἐπινοίας τὰ ὦτα δελεάζειν· ὧν ἐκ πολλοῦ τοῦ περιόντος οἱ Μωυσέως γνώριμοι, μεμαθηκότες ἐκ πρώτης ἡλικίας ἐρᾶν ἀληθείας, καταφρονοῦσιν ἀνεξαπάτητοι διατελοῦντες.
64 Ἀλλ' ἐπειδὴ τὰ διωνομασμένα συμπόσια τοιαύτης μεστὰ φλυαρίας ἐστίν, ἐν ἑαυτοῖς ἔχοντα τὸν ἔλεγχον, εἴ τις μὴ πρὸς δόξας καὶ τὴν διαδοθεῖσαν περὶ αὐτῶν ὡς δὴ πάνυ κατωρθωμένων φήμην ἐθελήσειεν ἀφορᾶν, ἀντιτάξω ⟨τὰ⟩ τῶν ἀνατεθεικότων τὸν ἴδιον βίον καὶ ἑαυτοὺς ἐπιστήμῃ καὶ θεωρίᾳ τῶν τῆς φύσεως πραγμάτων κατὰ τὰς τοῦ προφήτου Μωυσέως ἱερωτάτας ὑφηγήσεις.
65 οὗτοι τὸ μὲν πρῶτον ἀθροίζονται δι' ἑπτὰ ἑβδομάδων, οὐ μόνον τὴν ἁπλῆν ἑβδομάδα ἀλλὰ καὶ τὴν δύναμιν τεθηπότες· ἁγνὴν γὰρ

[17] On devotion to truth and the laws of Moses, see *Q.o.p.* 88; *War* 2. 145.

Appendix

swilled themselves full of strong wine, are, as if they had drunk, not wine, but some deranging and maddening potion, or any other drug more baleful still in its power of unseating the reason. And they yell and rage like wild dogs, and set upon and bite one another, nipping off one anothers' noses, ears and fingers and any other parts of the body; in such wise as to demonstrate the truth of the old story about Cyclops and the companions of Odysseus. For they devour, as the poet says, gobbets of human flesh, and with worse ferocity than he displayed.

* * * * *

There follows a very long account of contemporary secular banquets and of the symposia described by Plato and Xenophon. The practices at such feasts are denigrated.

* * * * *

I say nothing of the mythical figments, and monsters with two bodies; which to begin with, grew together by mutual attraction in one mass, and afterwards were separated, as if parts which had merely come together, owing to the dissolution of the bond which held them together. For all such stories as these easily lead men astray; as they can entice their ears by the novelty of the idea. But from a lofty vantage ground the disciples of Moses can despise such tales; and keep themselves free from the deception, having learned from their tenderest age to love the truth.[17]

However, since the banquets so widely known are infected with such folly, and so carry in themselves their own condemnation to any one who cares to have regard to anything except fashion and the glamour of their reputation for being entirely correct and faultless of their kind; I will contrast the banquets of those who have devoted their own life as well as themselves to knowledge and contemplation of the realities of nature, in accordance with the most holy counsels of the prophet Moses. These meet together for the first time after seven weeks, out of reverence not only for the simple seventh, but for its power as well. For they recognise its holy and eternally virgin character. But this meeting is

καὶ ἀειπάρθενον αὐτὴν ἴσασιν. ἔστι δὲ προέορτος μεγίστης ἑορτῆς, ἣν πεντηκοντὰς ἔλαχεν, ἁγιώτατος καὶ φυσικώτατος ἀριθμῶν, ἐκ τῆς τοῦ ὀρθογωνίου τριγώνου δυνάμεως, ὅπερ ἐστὶν ἀρχὴ τῆς τῶν ὅλων γενέσεως, συσταθείς.

66 Ἐπειδὰν οὖν συνέλθωσι λευχειμονοῦντες φαιδροὶ μετὰ τῆς ἀνωτάτω σεμνότητος, ὑποσημαίνοντός τινος τῶν ἐφημερευτῶν—οὕτω γὰρ ὀνομάζειν ἔθος τοὺς ἐν ταῖς τοιαύταις ὑπηρεσίαις—, πρὸ τῆς κατακλίσεως στάντες ἑξῆς κατὰ στοῖχον ἐν κόσμῳ καὶ τάς τε ὄψεις καὶ τὰς χεῖρας εἰς οὐρανὸν ἀνατείναντες, τὰς μὲν ἐπειδὴ τὰ θέας ἄξια καθορᾶν ἐπαιδεύθησαν, τὰς δὲ ὅτι καθαραὶ λημμάτων εἰσὶν ὑπ' οὐδεμιᾶς προφάσεως τῶν εἰς πορισμὸν μιαινόμεναι, προσεύχονται τῷ θεῷ θυμήρη γενέσθαι καὶ κατὰ νοῦν ἀπαντῆσαι

67 τὴν εὐωχίαν. μετὰ δὲ τὰς εὐχὰς οἱ πρεσβύτεροι κατακλίνονται ταῖς εἰσκρίσεσιν ἀκολουθοῦντες· πρεσβυτέρους δὲ οὐ τοὺς πολυετεῖς καὶ πολιοὺς νομίζουσιν {ἀλλ' ἔτι κομιδῇ νέους παῖδας}, ἐὰν ὀψὲ τῆς προαιρέσεως ἐρασθῶσιν, ἀλλὰ τοὺς ἐκ πρώτης ἡλικίας ἐνηβήσαντας καὶ ἐνακμάσαντας τῷ θεωρητικῷ μέρει φιλοσοφίας, ὃ δὴ

68 κάλλιστον καὶ θειότατόν ἐστι. συνεστιῶνται δὲ καὶ γυναῖκες, ὧν πλεῖσται γηραιαὶ παρθένοι, τὴν ἁγνείαν οὐκ ἀνάγκῃ, καθάπερ ἔνιαι τῶν παρ' Ἕλλησιν ἱερειῶν, διαφυλάξασαι μᾶλλον ἢ καθ' ἑκούσιον γνώμην, διὰ ζῆλον καὶ πόθον σοφίας, ᾗ συμβιοῦν σπουδάσασαι τῶν περὶ σῶμα ἡδονῶν ἠλόγησαν, οὐ θνητῶν ἐκγόνων ἀλλ' ἀθανάτων ὀρεχθεῖσαι, ἃ μόνη τίκτειν ἀφ' ἑαυτῆς οἷά τέ ἐστιν ἡ θεοφιλὴς ψυχή, σπείραντος εἰς αὐτὴν ἀκτῖνας νοητὰς τοῦ πατρός, αἷς δυνήσεται θεωρεῖν τὰ σοφίας δόγματα.

69 Διανενέμηται δὲ ἡ κατάκλισις χωρὶς μὲν ἀνδράσιν ἐπὶ δεξιά, χωρὶς δὲ γυναιξὶν ἐπ' εὐώνυμα. μή πού τις ὑπολαμβάνει στρωμνάς, εἰ καὶ οὐ πολυτελεῖς, ἀλλ' οὖν μαλακωτέρας ἀνθρώποις εὐγενέσι καὶ ἀστείοις καὶ φιλοσοφίας ἀσκηταῖς εὐτρεπίσθαι; στιβάδες γάρ εἰσιν εἰκαιοτέρας ὕλης, ἐφ' ὧν εὐτελῆ πάνυ χαμαίστρωτα παπύρου τῆς ἐγχωρίου, μικρὸν ὑπερέχοντα κατὰ τοὺς

---

[18] This festival is the Feast of Weeks or Pentecost. Compare 1QS 1-3; 5: 7-8.

[19] On the Pentecontad calendar, cf. the document in Cave 4 at Qumran referred to by Milik, *Ten Years of Discovery*, p. 92 and 11QTS 18-22 (see Yadin, *The Temple Scroll* I, pp. 116-22).

the eve-celebration of the greatest festival,[18] which the number fifty has had assigned to it, as being the most holy and natural of numbers,[19] being composed out of the power of the right-angled triangle, which is the source of the creation of the universe.

When, therefore, they have met in white raiment[20] and with cheerful aspect, yet with the deepest solemnity, one of the Ephemereutae (which is the name commonly given to those who perform these services) gives a sign; and before laying themselves down on the couches, they take their stand one after another in a row in orderly fashion, and upturn their eyes and outstretch their hands to heaven; their eyes, since they have been taught to behold things which merit to be seen; but their hands, because they are pure from unjust gains, being stained by nothing that might be regarded as money-getting. So standing they pray to God that their festivity may be pleasing in his sight and acceptable. But after the prayer, the Elders lie down, each in the order of his election into the society. For they do not regard as elders those who are aged and grey-headed; but, on the contrary, account these to be still mere infants, in case they have been late in embracing the vocation. Elders are, in their regard, those who from their earliest age[21] have passed their youth and maturity in the contemplative branch of philosophy, which truly is the noblest and most divine.[22] But women, also, join in the banquet, of whom most are aged virgins, that have preserved intact their chastity; not so much under constraint, like some priestesses among the Hellenes, as of their own free wills, and because of their zeal and longing for Wisdom; with whom they were anxious to live, and therefore despised the pleasures of the body. For they yearned not for mortal progeny, but for the immortal which the god-enamoured soul is alone able to bring forth of itself, because the father has sown into it rays of reason, whereby it can behold the principles of wisdom.[23]

But they do not lie down indiscriminately, but the men's couches are set apart on the right-hand side, and those of the women apart on the left. Perhaps some one imagines that couches, if not of a very expensive kind, yet, anyhow, fairly soft, have been got ready for persons who, like themselves, are nobly born and of goodly life and practisers of philosophy. Well, they are beds of a rude material, on which are laid

---

[20] On white clothes, cf. *War* 2. 123.

[21] For the presence of young men, see *War* 2. 120.

[22] Contrast to this praise of contemplation the picture of Essenes as active. See above, sect. 1; cf. *Q.o.p.* 76, 80; 1QS 6: 6–7; 8: 11–12.

[23] On celibacy, see *Apol.* 14–17; *War* 2. 121; *Ant.* 18. 21.

ἀγκῶνας, ἵνα ἐπερείδοιντο· τὴν μὲν γὰρ Λακωνικὴν σκληραγωγίαν ὑπανιᾶσιν, ἀεὶ δὲ καὶ πανταχοῦ τὴν ἐλευθέριον εὐκολίαν ἐπιτηδεύ-
70 ουσιν, ἀνὰ κράτος τοῖς ἡδονῆς φίλτροις ἀπεχθόμενοι. διακονοῦνται δὲ οὐχ ὑπ' ἀνδραπόδων, ἡγούμενοι συνόλως τὴν θεραπόντων κτῆσιν εἶναι παρὰ φύσιν· ἡ μὲν γὰρ ἐλευθέρους ἅπαντας γεγέννηκεν, αἱ δέ τινων ἀδικίαι καὶ πλεονεξίαι ζηλωσάντων τὴν ἀρχέκακον ἀνισότητα καταζεύξασαι τὸ ἐπὶ τοῖς ἀσθενεστέροις
71 κράτος τοῖς δυνατωτέροις ἀνῆψαν. ἐν δὴ τῷ ἱερῷ τούτῳ συμποσίῳ δοῦλος μὲν ὡς ἔφην οὐδείς, ἐλεύθεροι δὲ ὑπηρετοῦσι, τὰς διακονικὰς χρείας ἐπιτελοῦντες οὐ πρὸς βίαν οὐδὲ προστάξεις ἀναμένοντες, ἀλλ' ἐθελουσίῳ γνώμῃ φθάνοντες μετὰ σπουδῆς καὶ
72 προθυμίας τὰς ἐπικελεύσεις. οὐδὲ γὰρ οἱ τυχόντες ἐλεύθεροι τάττονται πρὸς ταῖς ὑπουργίαις ταύταις, ἀλλ' οἱ νέοι τῶν ἐν τῷ συστήματι μετὰ πάσης ἐπιμελείας ἀριστίνδην ἐπικριθέντες, ὃν χρὴ τρόπον ἀστείους καὶ εὐγενεῖς πρὸς ἄκραν ἀρετὴν ἐπειγομένους· οἳ καθάπερ υἱοὶ γνήσιοι φιλοτίμως ἄσμενοι πατράσι καὶ μητράσιν ὑπουργοῦσι, κοινοὺς αὑτῶν γονεῖς νομίζοντες οἰκειοτέρους τῶν ἀφ' αἵματος, εἴ γε καλοκἀγαθίας οὐδὲν οἰκειότερόν ἐστι τοῖς εὖ φρονοῦσιν· ἄζωστοι δὲ καὶ καθειμένοι τοὺς χιτωνίσκους εἰσίασιν ὑπηρετήσοντες, ἕνεκα τοῦ μηδὲν εἴδωλον ἐπιφέρεσθαι δουλοπρεποῦς σχήματος.

73 Εἰς τοῦτο τὸ συμπόσιον—οἶδ' ὅτι γελάσονταί τινες ἀκούσαντες, γελάσονται δὲ οἱ κλαυθμῶν καὶ θρήνων ἄξια δρῶντες—οἶνος ἐκείναις ταῖς ἡμέραις οὐκ εἰσκομίζεται, ἀλλὰ διαυγέστατον ὕδωρ, ψυχρὸν μὲν τοῖς πολλοῖς, θερμὸν δὲ τῶν πρεσβυτάτων τοῖς ἁβροδιαίτοις· καὶ τράπεζα καθαρὰ τῶν ἐναίμων, ἐφ' ἧς ἄρτοι μὲν τροφή, προσόψημα δὲ ἅλες, οἷς ἔστιν ὅτε καὶ ὕσσωπος ἥδυσμα
74 παραρτύεται διὰ τοὺς τρυφῶντας. νηφάλια γὰρ ὡς τοῖς ἱερεῦσι θύειν καὶ τούτοις βιοῦν ὁ ὀρθὸς λόγος ὑφηγεῖται· οἶνος μὲν γὰρ ἀφροσύνης φάρμακον, ὄψα δὲ πολυτελῆ τὸ θρεμμάτων ἀπληστότατον διερεθίζει, τὴν ἐπιθυμίαν.

75 Καὶ τὰ μὲν πρῶτα τοιαῦτα. μετὰ δὲ τὸ κατακλιθῆναι μὲν τοὺς συμπότας ἐν αἷς ἐδήλωσα τάξεσι, στῆναι δὲ τοὺς διακόνους ἐν

---

[24] On vegetarianism, contrast *Apol.* 8 and the animal bones carefully buried at Qumran.

very cheap palliasses made of the native papyrus, raised a little near the elbows in order that they may lean upon them. For they remit the harshness of the Laconic discipline; but practise always and everywhere the contentedness of true freedom, by opposing might and main the seductions of pleasure. And they are not waited on by slaves, because they deem any possession of servants whatever to be contrary to nature. For she hath begotten all men alike free; but the injustice and greedy oppression of some who were zealous for the inequality that is the source of all evil, laid a yoke on the weaker ones and gave the control into the hands of the stronger. In this holy banquet, then, there is, as I said, no slave; but the service is one of entire freedom, and they perform such service and waiting as is required, not under constraint nor even waiting for orders, but spontaneously, and even anticipate their orders by their careful and ready zeal. For it is not any and every free man who is appointed to discharge these duties, but the novices of the society chosen by merit in the most careful manner; as needs should be godly persons and noble, that are pressing on to win the heights of virtue. And these, like true sons, gladly submit to wait upon their fathers and mothers, and even covet it as an honour; for they regard them as their common parents, and as more their own than those who are so by blood; inasmuch as in the regard of those who are high-minded, nothing is more one's own and akin to oneself than true righteousness. And they go in to do the waiting with their chitons loose and not girt up, in order not to wear the least appearance of being slaves or of demeaning themselves as such.

Into this banquet—I know that some will make merry, when they hear of it. However only they will do so, whose own actions are matter for tears and lamentations—on the days in question wine is not brought to table, but the clearest and purest water; cold for the many, but warm for such of the more aged as are of a delicate habit of life. And the table is free from the animal food, which would pollute it;[24] and on it is set bread to eat, with salt as a relish; to which hyssop is sometimes added as a seasoning to sweeten it, for the sake of the luxurious among them. For right reason, as it counsels the priests to offer sober sacrifices, so it counsels these to live soberly. For wine is a drug of folly, and expensive viands arouse lust, the most insatiable of brute beasts.[25]

And such are the preliminaries. But after the banqueters have lain them down in the positions set forth by me, and while those who are

[25] On wine, contrast *War* 2. 132–3 and cf. 1QSa 2: 17–22; 1QS 6: 5.

κόσμῳ πρὸς ὑπηρεσίαν ἑτοίμους, ⟨ὁ πρόεδρος αὐτῶν, πολλῆς ἁπάντων ἡσυχίας γενομένης⟩—πότε δὲ οὐκ ἔστιν; εἴποι τις ἄν· ἀλλ' ἔτι μᾶλλον ἢ πρότερον, ὡς μηδὲ γρύξαι τινὰ τολμᾶν ἢ ἀναπνεῦσαι βιαιότερον—, ζητεῖ τι τῶν ἐν τοῖς ἱεροῖς γράμμασιν ἢ καὶ ὑπ' ἄλλου προταθὲν ἐπιλύεται, φροντίζων μὲν οὐδὲν ἐπιδείξεως—οὐ γὰρ τῆς ἐπὶ δεινότητι λόγων εὐκλείας ὀρέγεται—, θεάσασθαι δέ τινα ποθῶν ἀκριβέστερον καὶ θεασάμενος μὴ φθονῆσαι τοῖς εἰ καὶ μὴ ὁμοίως ὀξυδορκοῦσι, τὸν γοῦν τοῦ μαθεῖν

76 ἵμερον παραπλήσιον ἔχουσι. καὶ ὁ μὲν σχολαιοτέρᾳ χρῆται τῇ διδασκαλίᾳ, διαμέλλων καὶ βραδύνων ταῖς ἐπαναλήψεσιν, ἐγχαράττων ταῖς ψυχαῖς τὰ νοήματα—τῇ γὰρ ἑρμηνείᾳ τοῦ εὐτρόχως καὶ ἀπνευστὶ συνείροντος ὁ τῶν ἀκροωμένων νοῦς συνομαρτεῖν ἀδυνατῶν ὑστερίζει καὶ ἀπολείπεται τῆς καταλήψεως τῶν

77 λεγομένων—· οἱ δὲ ἀνωρθιακότες ⟨τὰ ὦτα καὶ τοὺς ὀφθαλμοὺς ἀνατετακότες⟩ εἰς αὐτὸν ἐπὶ μιᾶς καὶ τῆς αὐτῆς σχέσεως ἐπιμένοντες ἀκροῶνται, τὸ μὲν συνιέναι καὶ κατειληφέναι νεύματι καὶ βλέμματι διασημαίνοντες, τὸν δὲ ἔπαινον τοῦ λέγοντος ἱλαρότητι καὶ τῇ σχέδην περιαγωγῇ τοῦ προσώπου, τὴν δὲ διαπόρησιν ἠρεμαιοτέρᾳ κινήσει τῆς κεφαλῆς καὶ ἄκρῳ δακτύλῳ τῆς δεξιᾶς χειρός· οὐχ ἧττον δὲ τῶν κατακεκλιμένων οἱ παρεστῶ-

78 τες νέοι προσέχουσιν. αἱ δὲ ἐξηγήσεις τῶν ἱερῶν γραμμάτων γίνονται δι' ὑπονοιῶν ἐν ἀλληγορίαις· ἅπασα γὰρ ἡ νομοθεσία δοκεῖ τοῖς ἀνδράσι τούτοις ἐοικέναι ζῴῳ καὶ σῶμα μὲν ἔχειν τὰς ῥητὰς διατάξεις, ψυχὴν δὲ τὸν ἐναποκείμενον ταῖς λέξεσιν ἀόρατον νοῦν, ἐν ᾧ ἤρξατο ἡ λογικὴ ψυχὴ διαφερόντως τὰ οἰκεῖα θεωρεῖν, ὥσπερ διὰ κατόπτρου τῶν ὀνομάτων ἐξαίσια κάλλη νοημάτων ἐμφαινόμενα κατιδοῦσα καὶ τὰ μὲν σύμβολα διαπτύξασα καὶ διακαλύψασα, γυμνὰ δὲ εἰς φῶς προαγαγοῦσα τὰ ἐνθύμια τοῖς δυναμένοις ἐκ μικρᾶς ὑπομνήσεως τὰ ἀφανῆ διὰ τῶν φανερῶν

79 θεωρεῖν. ἐπειδὰν οὖν ἱκανῶς ὁ πρόεδρος διειλέχθαι δοκῇ καὶ κατὰ προαίρεσιν ἀπηντηκέναι τῷ μὲν ἡ διάλεξις εὐσκόπως ταῖς ἐπιβολαῖς, τοῖς δὲ ἡ ἀκρόασις, κρότος ἐξ ἁπάντων ὡς ἂν

---

[26] See 1QS 7: 15 for a prohibition on using the left hand for this purpose.

Appendix

serving stand in due order ready for service; their president, when silence has been established all round—and when is there anything but silence? some one will ask;—anyhow there is now a deeper silence than before, such that no one ventures to mutter or even take a loud breath—the president, I say, then, examines some text in the scriptures, or explains one that has been put forward by another. And, in doing so, he does not concern himself to make a parade of his learning; for he does not aspire to the reputation which is earned by cleverness in discussion. But he simply desires to see for himself certain things with fair exactitude, and having seen them to be in no wise grudging towards those who, even if they are not as sharp-sighted as himself, have at any rate as earnest a desire to learn. And so he proceeds in a leisurely way with his instruction, lingering and going slowly over the points; and, by recapitulating them, impresses them on their souls. For if he ran on, and without pausing for breath made a rigmarole of his exposition, the mind of his audience would find itself incapable of keeping pace with him, and falling behind would miss the drift of his remarks. But they have their ears pricked up and their eyes fixed on him and remain in one and the same attitude as they listen; signifying by a nod or a look that they understand and have taken in his meaning, and by their cheerfulness and by slightly turning their faces about their praise of the speaker; while perplexity they show by a very gentle movement of the head and with a finger-tip of the right hand.[26] But the younger members who stand by attend to the discourse no less than those who have lain down. But the exposition of sacred writ proceeds by unfolding the meaning hidden in allegories. For the entire law is regarded by these persons as resembling an animal; and for its body it has the literal precepts, but for its soul the unseen reason (or *nous*) hidden away in the words. And in and through this reason the rational and self-conscious soul begins to contemplate in a special manner its own proper intuitions. For by means of the names, as it were by means of a gazing crystal, it discerns the surpassing beauties of the notions conveyed in them. Thus, on the one hand, it unfolds and unveils the symbols, and on the other brings forward the meanings into the light and exhibits them naked to those who by a little exercise of memory are able to behold things not clear by means of things that are. So soon, therefore, as the president seems to have discoursed long enough, and when his discourse is judged by him in accordance with his purpose to have met fairly the objects aimed at, while at the same time they as listeners have been satisfied; then, as if all were delighted together, hands are clapped all round in the expectation

80 συνηδομένων εἰς τὸ ἔτι ἐψόμενον γίνεται. καὶ ἔπειτα ὁ μὲν ἀναστὰς ὕμνον ᾄδει πεποιημένον εἰς τὸν θεόν, ἢ καινὸν αὐτὸς πεποιηκὼς ἢ ἀρχαῖόν τινα τῶν πάλαι ποιητῶν—μέτρα γὰρ καὶ μέλη καταλελοίπασι πολλὰ ἐπῶν τριμέτρων, προσοδίων ὕμνων, παρασπονδείων, παραβωμίων, στασίμων χορικῶν στροφαῖς πολυστρόφοις εὖ διαμεμετρημένων—, μεθ' ὃν καὶ οἱ ἄλλοι κατὰ τάξεις ἐν κόσμῳ προσήκοντι, πάντων κατὰ πολλὴν ἡσυχίαν ἀκροωμένων, πλὴν
81 ὁπότε τὰ ἀκροτελεύτια καὶ ἐφύμνια ᾄδειν δέοι· τότε γὰρ ἐξηχοῦσι πάντες τε καὶ πᾶσαι. ὅταν δὲ ἕκαστος διαπεράνηται τὸν ὕμνον, οἱ νέοι τὴν πρὸ μικροῦ λεχθεῖσαν τράπεζαν εἰσκομίζουσιν, ἐφ' ἧς τὸ παναγέστατον σιτίον, ἄρτος ἐζυμωμένος μετὰ προσοψήματος ἁλῶν, οἷς ὕσσωπος ἀναμέμικται, δι' αἰδὼ τῆς ἀνακειμένης ἐν τῷ ἁγίῳ προνάῳ ἱερᾶς τραπέζης· ἐπὶ γὰρ ταύτης εἰσὶν ἄρτοι καὶ ἅλες ἄνευ ἡδυσμάτων, ἄζυμοι μὲν οἱ ἄρτοι, ἀμιγεῖς δὲ οἱ ἅλες.
82 προσῆκον γὰρ ἦν τὰ μὲν ἁπλούστατα καὶ εἰλικρινέστατα τῇ κρατίστῃ τῶν ἱερέων ἀπονεμηθῆναι μερίδι λειτουργίας ἆθλον, τοὺς δὲ ἄλλους τὰ μὲν ὅμοια ζηλοῦν, ἀπέχεσθαι δὲ τῶν αὐτῶν, ἵνα ἔχωσι προνομίαν οἱ κρείττονες.
83 Μετὰ δὲ τὸ δεῖπνον τὴν ἱερὰν ἄγουσι παννυχίδα. ἄγεται δὲ ἡ παννυχὶς τὸν τρόπον τοῦτον· ἀνίστανται πάντες ἁθρόοι, καὶ κατὰ μέσον τὸ συμπόσιον δύο γίνονται τὸ πρῶτον χοροί, ὁ μὲν ἀνδρῶν, ὁ δὲ γυναικῶν· ἡγεμὼν δὲ καὶ ἔξαρχος αἱρεῖται καθ' ἑκάτερον
84 ἐντιμότατός τε καὶ ἐμμελέστατος. εἶτα ᾄδουσι πεποιημένους ὕμνους εἰς τὸν θεὸν πολλοῖς μέτροις καὶ μέλεσι, τῇ μὲν συνηχοῦντες, τῇ δὲ καὶ ἀντιφώνοις ἁρμονίαις ἐπιχειρονομοῦντες καὶ ἐπορχούμενοι, καὶ ἐπιθειάζοντες τοτὲ μὲν τὰ προσόδια, τοτὲ δὲ τὰ στάσιμα, στροφάς τε τὰς ἐν χορείᾳ καὶ ἀντιστροφὰς ποιού-
85 μενοι. εἶτα ὅταν ἑκάτερος τῶν χορῶν ἰδίᾳ καὶ καθ' ἑαυτὸν ἑστιαθῇ, καθάπερ ἐν ταῖς βακχείαις ἀκράτου σπάσαντες τοῦ θεοφιλοῦς, ἀναμίγνυνται καὶ γίνονται χορὸς εἷς ἐξ ἀμφοῖν, μίμημα τοῦ πάλαι συστάντος κατὰ τὴν ἐρυθρὰν θάλασσαν ἕνεκα τῶν θαυματουργ-
86 ηθέντων ἐκεῖ. τὸ γὰρ πέλαγος προστάξει θεοῦ τοῖς μὲν σωτηρίας αἴτιον τοῖς δὲ πανωλεθρίας γίνεται· ῥαγέντος μὲν γὰρ καὶ βιαίοις ἀνακοπαῖς ὑποσυρέντος καὶ ἑκατέρωθεν ἐξ ἐναντίας οἷα τειχῶν παγέντων, τὸ μεθόριον διάστημα εἰς λεωφόρον ὁδὸν καὶ ξηρὰν

---

[27] Compare 1QSa 2: 17–21 and cf. the *Hodayot* at Qumran.

of what is still to come. After which the one of them stands up and sings a hymn composed in honour of God; either a new one which he has made himself or some old one of the poets that were long ago. For these have left measures and many melodies of poetry in triple measure, of professional hymns, hymns for the libation, hymns at the altar, hymns of station or of the dance, deftly proportioned for turning and returning. After him, each one also of the rest sings, according to his rank, in due order,[27] while all listen in profound silence, except when it is time to sing the catches and refrains; for then they give out their voices in unison, all the men and all the women together. But when every one has finished his hymn, the novices bring in the table just now described, on which is the all-purest food, namely, bread leavened with a relish of salt, with which hyssop has been mixed, out of reverence for the holy table of offering in the sacred vestibule of the temple. For on this there are loaves and salt, without any seasoning to sweeten it. The loaves are unleavened, and the salt also is unmixed. For it is meet that the simplest and purest things should be reserved for the highest class of priests as a reward for their service in the temple; but that the rest should aspire to a portion that is similar, yet abstain from one that is the same, in order that their superiors may keep their privilege.[28]

But after the feast is over, they celebrate the holy all-night festival; and this is kept in the following manner:—All rise together, and in the middle of the banquet there are formed, at first, two choruses, one of men, the other of women, and a guide and leader is chosen on either side who is one most held in honour and most suitable. Then they sing hymns composed in honour of God in many measures and strains, sometimes singing in unison, and sometimes waving their hands in time with antiphonal harmonies, and leaping up, and uttering inspired cries, as they either move in procession or stand still, making the turns and counter-turns proper to the dance. Then, when each of the choirs has had its fill of dancing by itself and separate from the other, as if it were a Bacchic festival in which they had drunk deep of the Divine love, they unite, and form a single choir out of the two, in imitation of the dance long ago instituted by the side of the Red Sea to celebrate the miracles there wrought. For the sea, at the Divine behest, became to the one side a cause of salvation, but to the other of utter destruction. For the sea was rent asunder, and, with forced recoil, withdrew from its depths; and walls, as it were, of water were congealed on either hand over against

---

[28] On the communal meal, cf. in general *Q.o.p.* 86; *War* 2. 130–2.

πᾶσαν ἀνατμηθὲν εὐρύνετο, δι' ἧς ὁ λεὼς ἐπέζευσεν ἄχρι τῆς ἀντιπέραν ἠπείρου πρὸς τὰ μετέωρα παραπεμφθείς· ἐπιδραμόντος δὲ ταῖς παλιρροίαις καὶ τοῦ μὲν ἔνθεν τοῦ δὲ ἔνθεν εἰς τὸ χερσωθὲν ἔδαφος ἀναχυθέντος, οἱ ἐπακολουθήσαντες τῶν πολεμίων κατα-
87 κλυσθέντες διαφθείρονται. τοῦτο δὲ ἰδόντες καὶ παθόντες, ὃ λόγου καὶ ἐννοίας καὶ ἐλπίδος μεῖζον ἔργον ἦν, ἐνθουσιῶντές τε ἄνδρες ὁμοῦ καὶ γυναῖκες, εἷς γενόμενοι χορός, τοὺς εὐχαριστηρίους ὕμνους εἰς τὸν σωτῆρα θεὸν ᾖδον, ἐξάρχοντος τοῖς μὲν ἀνδράσι Μωυσέως τοῦ προφήτου, ταῖς δὲ γυναιξὶ Μαριὰμ τῆς προφήτιδος.
88 Τούτῳ μάλιστα ἀπεικονισθεὶς ὁ τῶν θεραπευτῶν καὶ θεραπευτρίδων, μέλεσιν ἀντήχοις καὶ ἀντιφώνοις πρὸς βαρὺν ἦχον τῶν ἀνδρῶν ὁ γυναικῶν ὀξὺς ἀνακιρνάμενος, ἐναρμόνιον συμφωνίαν ἀποτελεῖ καὶ μουσικὴν ὄντως· πάγκαλα μὲν τὰ νοήματα, πάγκαλοι δὲ αἱ λέξεις, σεμνοὶ δὲ οἱ χορευταί· τὸ δὲ τέλος καὶ τῶν νοημάτων
89 καὶ τῶν λέξεων καὶ τῶν χορευτῶν εὐσέβεια. μεθυσθέντες οὖν ἄχρι πρωΐας τὴν καλὴν ταύτην μέθην, οὐ καρηβαροῦντες ἢ καταμύοντες, ἀλλὰ διεγηγερμένοι μᾶλλον ἢ ὅτε παρεγένοντο εἰς τὸ συμπόσιον, τάς τε ὄψεις καὶ ὅλον τὸ σῶμα πρὸς τὴν ἕω στάντες, ἐπὰν θεάσωνται τὸν ἥλιον ἀνίσχοντα, τὰς χεῖρας ἀνατείναντες εἰς οὐρανὸν εὐημερίαν καὶ ἀλήθειαν ἐπεύχονται καὶ ὀξυωπίαν λογισμοῦ· καὶ μετὰ τὰς εὐχὰς εἰς τὰ ἑαυτῶν ἕκαστος σεμνεῖα ἀναχωροῦσι, πάλιν τὴν συνήθη φιλοσοφίαν ἐμπορευσόμενοι καὶ γεωργήσοντες.
90 Θεραπευτῶν μὲν δὴ πέρι τοσαῦτα θεωρίαν ἀσπασαμένων φύσεως καὶ τῶν ἐν αὐτῇ καὶ ψυχῇ μόνῃ βιωσάντων, οὐρανοῦ μὲν καὶ κόσμου πολιτῶν, τῷ δὲ πατρὶ καὶ ποιητῇ τῶν ὅλων γνησίως συσταθέντων ὑπ' ἀρετῆς, ἥτις ⟨θεοῦ⟩ φιλίαν αὐτοῖς προυξένησεν οἰκειότατον γέρας καλοκἀγαθίας προσθεῖσα, πάσης ἄμεινον εὐτυχίας, ἐπ' αὐτὴν ἀκρότητα φθάνον εὐδαιμονίας.

one another, in such wise that through the intervening space there was cut a broad highroad, and dry throughout to walk upon; and by it the host walked upon dry land unto the opposite continent, and were brought through in safety unto the rising ground. But then the sea ran in with the returning tide and from either side passed over the ground that had been made dry land. And straightway those of the enemy which had followed were overwhelmed and were destroyed. But when they both saw and experienced this mighty work, greater than could be told of, or thought of, or hoped for, men and women, all alike, were rapt with the Divine spirit, and, forming themselves into a single choir, sang hymns of thanksgiving unto God, Moses the prophet leading off the men and Miriam the prophetess the women.

In closest imitation whereof the choir of Therapeutae, male and female, has formed itself, and, as the deep tones of the men mingle with the shriller ones of the women in answering and antiphonal strains, a full and harmonious symphony results, and one that is veritably musical. Noble are the thoughts, and noble the words of their hymn, yea, and noble the choristers. But the end and aim of thought and words and choristers alike is holiness. When, then, they have made themselves drunk until dawn with this godly drunkenness, neither heavy of head nor with winking eyes, but more wide awake than when they came in unto the banquet, they stand up, and turn both their eyes and their whole bodies towards the East. And, so soon as they espy the sun rising, they stretch out aloft their hands to heaven and fall to praying for a fair day, and for truth, and for clear judgment to see with.[29] And after their prayers they retire each to his own sanctuary, to traffic in and cultivate afresh their customary philosophy.

Concerning the Therapeutae, then, let so much suffice, who embraced the contemplation of nature and of her verities, and lived a life of the soul alone. They truly are citizens of heaven and of the universe, and have been commended to the Father and Creator of all things by virtue, which secures unto them God's love; adding therein the only meet reward of godliness—better than any mere good fortune, because it lifts them in advance straight to the zenith of bliss.

---

[29] See above, sect. 27, and cf. *War* 2. 128.

BIBLIOGRAPHY

I. Pre-Qumran Literature

Frankel, Z., 'Die Essäer nach talmudischen Quellen', MGWJ 2 (1853), pp. 30–40, 61–73.

Hilgenfeld, A., *Die jüdische Apokalyptik in ihrer geschichtlichen Entwicklung* (1857), pp. 243–86.

Ginsburg, C. D., *The Essenes. Their History and Doctrines* (1864).

Lucius, P. E., *Der Essenismus in seinem Verhältniss zum Judenthum* (1881).

Hilgenfeld, A., *Ketzergeschichte des Urchristenthums* (1884), pp. 87–149.

Conybeare, F. C., *Philo about the Contemplative Life* (1895).

Wendland, P., 'Die Therapeuten und die philonische Schrift vom beschaulichen Leben', *Jahrbuch f. class. Philologie*, Suppl. 22 (1896), pp. 695–772.

Zeller, E., *Die Philosophie der Griechen* (1903), III.2, pp. 307–84.

Friedländer, M., *Die religiösen Bewegungen innerhalb des Judenthums im Zeitalter Jesu* (1905), pp. 114–68.

Kohler, K., 'Essenes', JE V, pp. 224–32.

Schürer, E., *Geschichte des jüdischen Volkes im Zeitalter Jesu Christi* II (1907), pp. 651–80.

Bauer, W., 'Essener', RE Suppl. IV, cols. 386–443.

Lightley, J. W., *Jewish Sects and Parties in the Time of Jesus* (1925), pp. 267–322.

Lévy, I., *La légende de Pythagore de Grèce en Palestine* (1927), pp. 231–4, 264–93.

Marchal, L., 'Esséniens', DBS II, cols. 1190–1232.

Heinemann, I., 'Therapeutai', RE Va, cols. 2321–46.

Thomas, J., *Le mouvement baptiste en Palestine et Syrie* (1935), pp. 4–32.

II. Post-Qumran Literature

Dupont-Sommer, A., *Aperçus préliminaires sur les manuscrits de la Mer Morte* (1950), pp. 105–17. [E.T. *The Dead Sea Scrolls: A Preliminary Survey* (1952), pp. 85–96.]

Brownlee, W. H., 'A Comparison of the Covenanters of the Dead Sea Scrolls with pre-Christian Jewish Sects', BA (1950), pp. 50–72.

Vermes, G. *Les manuscrits du désert de Juda* (1953), pp. 57–66. [E.T. *Discovery in the Judean Desert* (1956), pp. 52–61.]

Black, M., 'The Account of the Essenes in Hippolytus and Josephus', in C. H. Dodd Festschrift (1956), pp. 172-5.
Rabin, C., 'Yaḥad, Ḥaburah and Essenes', *Sukenik Memorial Volume* (1957), pp. 104-22 (Hebrew).
Cross, F. M., *The Ancient Library of Qumran and Modern Biblical Studies* (1958/1980), pp. 52-79.
Smith, M., 'The Description of the Essenes in Josephus and the Philosophoumena', HUCA 29 (1958), pp. 273-313.
Grelot, P., 'L'eschatologie des Esséniens et le livre d'Hénoch', RQ 1 (1958), pp. 113-31.
Medico, H. del, *Le mythe des Esséniens des origines à la fin du moyen âge* (1958).
Roth, C., 'Why the Qumran Sectaries cannot have been Essenes?', RQ 1 (1959), pp. 417-22.
id., 'Were the Qumran Sectaries Essenes?', JTS 10 (1959), pp. 87-93.
Milik, J. T., *Ten Years of Discovery in the Wilderness of Judaea* (1959), pp. 44-128.
Geoltrain, P., 'Esséniens et Hellénistes', ThZ 15 (1959), pp. 241-54.
Simon, M., *Les sectes juives au temps de Jésus* (1960), pp. 42-73, 105-13.
Wagner, S., *Die Essener in der wissenschaftlichen Discussion* (1960).
Vermes, G., 'The Etymology of Essenes', RQ 2 (1960), 427-43. [PBJS, pp. 8-29.]
Audet, J.-P., 'Qumrân et la notice de Pline sur les Esséniens', RB 68 (1961), pp. 346-87.
Dupont-Sommer, A., *The Essene Writings from Qumran* (1961).
Black, M. *The Essene Problem* (1961).
id., *The Scrolls and Christian Origins* (1961).
Farmer, W. R., 'Essenes', IDB II, pp. 143-9.
Laperrousaz, E. M., 'Infra hos Engadda', RB 69 (1962), 369-80.
Burchard, C., 'Pline et les Esséniens', RB 69 (1962), pp. 533-69.
Vermes, G., 'Essenes and Therapeutai', RQ 3 (1962), pp. 495-504. [PBJS, 30-36.]
Talmon, S., 'A Further Link between the Judaean Covenanters and the Essenes', HTR 56 (1963), pp. 313-19.
Nikiprowetzky, V., 'Les suppliants chez Philon d'Alexandrie', REJ 2 (1963), pp. 241-78.
Driver, G. R., *The Judaean Scrolls: The Problem and a Solution* (1965), pp. 100-24.
Black, M., 'The Tradition of the Hassidaean-Essene Asceticism', in *Colloque de Strasbourg* (1965), pp. 19-32.

Burchard, C., 'Solin et les Esséniens', in *Philon D'Alexandrie. Lyon 1966* (1967), pp. 392–407.

Baumgarten, J. M., 'The Essene Avoidance of Oil and the Laws of Purity', RQ 6 (1967), pp. 183–92.

Negoïtsa, A., 'Did the Essenes survive the 66–71 War?', RQ 6 (1969), pp. 517–30.

Braun, H., *Spätjüdisch-häretischer und früchristlicher Radikalismus. Jesus von Nazareth und die essenische Qumransekte* (1969), pp. 67–89.

Albright, W. F. and Mann, C. S., 'Qumran and the Essenes', in *The Scrolls and Christianity*, ed. M. Black (1969), pp. 11–25.

Vellas, B., 'Zur Etymologie des Namens *Essaiaoi*', ZAW 81 (1969), pp. 94–100.

Mansoor, M., 'Essenes', Enc. Jud. 6, cols. 899–902.

Guillaumont, A., 'A propos du célibat des Esséniens', in *Hommages à A. Dupont-Sommer* (1971), pp. 395–404.

Marx, A., 'Les racines du célibat essénien', RQ 7 (1971), pp. 323–42.

Adam A. and Burchard, C., *Antike Berichte über die Essener* (1972).

Murphy-O'Connor, J., 'The Essenes and their History', RB 81 (1974), pp. 215–44.

Hengel, M., *Judaism and Hellenism* (1974), pp. 218–47.

Murphy-O'Connor, J., 'The Essenes in Palestine', BA 40 (1977), pp. 106–24.

Vermes, G., *The Dead Sea Scrolls: Qumran in Perspective* (1977/1982).

Delcor, M. (ed.), *Qumrân. Sa piété, sa théologie, son milieu* (1978).

Schürer, E., Vermes G., Millar F., Black, M., *The History of the Jewish People in the Age of Jesus Christ* II (1979), pp. 555–597.

Mendels, D., 'Hellenistic Utopia and the Essenes', HTR 72 (1979), pp. 207–22.

Golb, N., 'The Problem of Origin and Identification of the Dead Sea Scrolls', PAAJR 124 (1980), pp. 1–24.

Dupont-Sommer, A., 'Essénisme et Bouddhisme', CRAI (1981), pp. 698–715.

Vermes, G., 'The Essenes and History', JJS 32 (1981), pp. 18–31.

Goranson, S., 'Essenes: Etymology from '*sh*'', RQ 11 (1984), pp. 483–98.

Qimron, E. and Strugnell, J., 'An Unpublished Halakhic Letter from Qumran', in *Biblical Archaeology Today* (1985), 400–7.

Lemaire, A., 'L'enseignement essénien et l'école de Qumrân', in *Hommage à V. Nikiprowetzky* (1986), pp. 191–203.

Davies, P. R., *Behind the Essenes: History and Ideology in the Dead Sea Scrolls* (1987).

Beall, T. S., *Josephus' Description of the Essenes illustrated by the Dead Sea Scrolls* (1988).